BANGKOK GAMBLE

BOOKS BY TOM CROWLEY

The Matt Chance Thrillers
Viper's Tail
Murder in the Slaughterhouse
Bangkok Gamble

Non-Fiction
Bangkok Pool Blues
Shrapnel Wounds
Stilwell's Retreat
Mayhem in Burma

TOM CROWLEY

BANGKOK GAMBLE
A Matt Chance Thriller

Down & Out Books
3959 Van Dyke Road, Suite 265
Lutz, FL 33558
DownAndOutBooks.com

Cover design by Alex Nauert

ISBN: 1-64396-153-5
ISBN-13: 978-1-64396-153-8

This book is dedicated to Gordon Maxwell
and the men of A Squadron, 25th Dragoons who served
so valiantly in the combat in the "Admin Box"
in Burma through the winter and spring of 1944.

You are not forgotten.

ACT I
CHAPTER ONE

She had escaped.

That was the important point. She had to forget the negatives or they would overwhelm her. The dirt road stretched before her into the night and on into the countryside, lined by palm trees. Shadows dotted the road from the dim moonlight above the trees. The tall rice stalks in the paddies behind the trees were bending slightly with the breeze. There were no lights or signs of habitation other than the temple grounds from which she had just fled.

She was sweating through the white robe they had made her wear, except for when one of the elect was using her. They had used her so often, letting her 'serve the elect' as they termed it. God, what if she was pregnant? She hurt from the beatings dealt to her for resisting. The pain was not just in one place but all over her body.

She was alone. Her mind frantically tried to come up with more facts to describe her situation. She thought organizing the facts in her mind would somehow help her to control her fear.

Okay, that was another fact. She was so scared she couldn't stop shaking as she ran. She couldn't let them catch her and take her back to that cell, to that depraved 'service center' as the religious brethren termed it.

She stumbled and ran. The wet cloak of the humid night air enveloped her. She had no plan except to get as far away as she could. She had to find people, farmers, anyone who could help her and hide her.

Her foot slipped in a hole in the road that had been covered by the tree shadows. She fell and scraped her knee, loose pebbles ground into her palms as she tried to break her fall. Ignore the pain, get up, keep moving.

Then beyond a bend in the road, beyond some trees, she glimpsed some farm huts and faint lights inside. The farmers would be simple people but they would see her need. They would help her.

She ran on. As she approached the huts she saw a small group of farmers gathered outside talking. They had their backs to her. She ran closer, calling to them. Just as she neared them, and slowed to a walk, they heard her and turned towards her. She was saved. They would protect her.

Then, as she came closer to the group, their circle opened, she saw who it was the villagers had been talking to. Facing her were two of the senior monks, including Uncle Pham, one who had used her often. She stopped, tried to turn, but instead, exhausted, fell to her knees, sobbing.

Uncle Pham smiled at her but with his mouth only, not his snake- eyes which seemed to look right though her with contempt.

"Little sister, we were worried about you. It's okay now. We'll take care of you as we promised. We're here to take you home."

The farmers didn't look at her. Most had already turned and were walking back towards their thatched roof homes.

CHAPTER TWO

He stood outside the car for a second and surveyed the nightclub. Foreigners and Thai women were flocking through the doors. He could feel the bass throbbing as he stood outside. It was a scene he had scouted several times previously, but tonight it all felt different. There was a tension in the air that he understood, it vibrated from his more aware consciousness. He and his partner had a mission tonight. Just stay in the moment, he thought. Follow your training. Serve the revered one.

The heat of the night didn't bother him. Amnat had grown used to much worse in his years of child apprenticeship, isolated and abused in a country temple. He turned and nodded to the limo driver. Go ahead and park. He held up five fingers. They would be out in five minutes.

His fellow acolyte, somewhat shorter than he, was dressed the same, in all black, slacks, T-shirt and loose jacket. Both of their heads were shaved, eyebrows too. He looked at his partner and nodded. It was time to bring her in. They headed towards the door; a fat, but still well-muscled, doorman squinted at them for a second before quickly stepping back. The doorman was not a follower of the venerable one, but he knew not to interfere with the two disciples.

Inside they stepped sideways, trying to stay out of the main traffic flow and the distorted whirl of colored lights, which seemed to be pulsing to the rhythm of the music. They stayed out of direct view of the bouncing, vibrating, drunken, drugged, lust-ridden crowd. It was not a new scene. Their duty had taken them here as well as other busy night scenes over the past year. It was where the young girls went and it was the young girls they were after. Not the whores but special ones, the so-called Bangkok 'hi-so girls.' Beautiful young girls from families of wealth.

Amnat punched his companion in the arm and nodded towards the back of the bar, a small open area just off the dance floor and near the toilets in back. The girl was standing there with her girlfriend, talking with two foreigners. These men were possibly the girls' companions for the night. They were young men, models probably as that is what the girls seemed to prefer. He shook his head in disgust, of course they were near the toilets, they needed a convenient place to take their drugs. Gifts from the foreign boys. It was a small price for the foreigners to pay to satisfy the girls' needs. The girls would return the favor later on with a sexual abandon well stimulated by the drugs. Currently the drugs of choice were ecstasy (known as Ya-E locally) and a bit of Special K, which prolonged the Ya-E hit. No amphetamines or Ice. Those were the drugs of the sex workers, used in order for them to sustain their frantic pace and multiple customers all night.

The girls turned to talk to each other, heads almost touching for a minute, and the men walked away. Then one of the girls headed towards the woman's toilet. Time for the drugs. She was not the one they wanted. The one they wanted was left alone, possibly she had already had her hit as she seemed a bit unsteady standing there. He looked at his partner and nodded. No words were needed. It was time to collect the new girl for the temple master, Leung Somboon. The man who had saved them, the man who understood the painful, shameful past they had endured as children, the man who had given them hope and a mission in life. The girl would learn to serve the temple in her own special way.

Lek closed the door to the women's toilet, pushing it back with her rump. She was eager to score. She leaned against the wall next to the door. It seemed she could feel the wall moving with the insistent throbbing of the music. The lights were bright, brighter than she wanted, but the girls needed good light to adjust their makeup didn't they? There were four stalls and one opened just as she leaned against the wall. The girl came out, gave her a quick glance, looked after her makeup in the mirror and moved quickly out the door.

She had the pill in her hand, ready to throw it into her mouth, when the door opened on another stall and the girl walked out. The girl looked anxiously at Lek, was something wrong? It was none of her business. The girl repeated her routine, checked her makeup, made an adjustment and moved out the door.

Lek felt alive in anticipation of the rush. Her blood pounded through her veins. She looked down at the Ya-E, the ecstasy, a round pink pill tonight, would be the first she would take. She quickly gulped it down followed by a sip from the drink she had carried. She leaned back against the wall again. It would take a few minutes, but now she felt she had time.

Another girl came through the door, looked at Lek standing there, and went to one of the stalls. Lek unfolded the small paper packet with just a touch of Special K, ketamine powder, and poured it into her mouth. Just a touch of Special K Oi had warned her. It'll boost you quickly. You don't want to be a zombie. It was going to be a good night. She wanted to remember it but she didn't want to waste a good drug. She washed all the powder down with a quick drink and laid back against the wall. Things would slow down soon.

It would be a good night. She felt really good. She decided

5

she would take a minute and just enjoy the feeling of the drugs moving through her. Then she had to go find the guy who would complete the party for her.

Oi was getting impatient waiting for Lek. She waited next to the crowded dance floor. The drugs were already coursing through her veins. The lights were whirling faster. She was moving to the music, hands in the air above her head. She could feel everything. She felt a drop of sweat moving down her sternum between her breasts. It was animal time. She needed the male connection to top things off but the boys had walked away for a second while Lek was getting her fix.

She was so into the sound, into the lights, into her body, moving her body in the sensual mating motions that excited the boys, that she didn't notice the two dark skinned Thai guys walking towards her until the last second. They spoke to her but everything, the lights, the music, it all seemed a bit distorted now. She didn't understand what they were saying or really hear it. The big one's eyes were fixed on her and his mouth was moving. Maybe she had taken a bit too much Special K. They were reaching out for her, each taking one of her arms. She felt lethargic. She couldn't move.

Holding her left arm firmly, Amnat turned to move out along the side of the wall where the crowd was thinner. He led the way with the girl. His partner followed close behind gently holding her right arm. Thanks to the drugs nothing more was needed. Those who saw them instinctively moved back. Besides being dressed all in black, they were country boys, dark skinned, black coffee not cafe au lait, in a town and a nightclub group that worshipped white skin. The fact that they were completely shaven added an ominous touch to their appearance.

He slowly steered her back the way they had come in. No

one interfered. It was just another stoned rich girl being shown out of the club. It was a periodic ritual in a club such as this. The music continued to pound. He was sweating now. The heat of the packed mass inside the club affecting even him.

He nodded to the doorman who held the door open for them while looking over their heads to the inside of the club for any sign of trouble. There was none. The car was waiting. He put the girl in the back seat and joined her there with his arm around her shoulders. Oi slumped against him. She was awake but felt no urge to resist. It was the Special K taking effect.

"It's okay little sister. We're here to take you home."

They were taking her to her new home. Her new life, one she wouldn't want to know about in advance, would begin when next she awoke. She would find it much more taxing than her college schedule.

CHAPTER THREE

Bangkok had been Matt Chance's home for several years now. There were some less desirable parts of Bangkok he hadn't visited yet. The Tao Poon gambling fortress was one of them.

Apprehension and curiosity competed for emotional control as he walked up the center of the alleyway, dodging fast moving motorbikes as he went. There were pools of rainwater collected in the street, at least he hoped it was rainwater. Whatever it was hadn't been enough to cool things off. He could feel the waves of heat coming up from broken cement. There was still rainwater dripping from the edges of the roofs and edging out of drainpipes on the ground. It was a poor man's sauna. Wearing his usual outfit of cargo pants, a polo shirt and hiking shoes he didn't fit the usual image of the everyday Chinese gambler. Stay alert! He ran his eyes along the roof lines. Fallujah had taught him that, it was his patrol routine, eyes up, scan the upper balconies, and the roof lines. That's where the ambush would come from, if it didn't come from the IED hidden in the street trash.

People were glancing at him from the balconies and doorways. There were several rough-looking goons to be passed along the way and Matt got some hard looks but nobody stopped him or questioned him.

Though born and raised in Bangkok, the child of an ill-fated love match between a Thai woman and an American CIA agent, Matt had gone to college in the U.S. Nearly ten years of service in the U.S. Army had followed the schooling, mostly as a member of the 75th Ranger Regiment. He had seen combat in both Iraq and Afghanistan but it wasn't the combat that had driven him out of the service. He had loved the Ranger ethos and the men he served with but he had come to hate the narrow minded 'get your ticket punched' career drive of many senior officers in both the Rangers and support units. Their self-absorbed focus on their career promotion paths often seemed to undermine the courageous efforts of the Rangers who went 'outside the wire.' After being wounded in action, Matt spent several months in the hospital which gave him time to reflect. He decided to get out of the service and return home to Thailand.

He had contacts in both the Thai military and police through Thai officers he had met and helped during the Ranger course years before. Now, back home, he had come to be known as a man to call on when a friend was in trouble. That was what had brought him here to Tao Poon today. The man who called him, the Thai gambler and bar owner, Jack, was not really a friend but a contact. Matt knew him from one of the pool bars Jack owned, which was where Jack did most of his personal gambling with friends. Matt was there for the pool, not the gambling, but still he had developed a polite relationship with Jack. Thus he had come here in response to Jack's plea for help and a meeting to discuss the problem. Also he admitted to himself he was curious to see the notorious Tao Poon complex up close.

He looked up the narrow alley that led into Tao Poon centered on an imposing five-story, not so grand, stone palace. In any other city it would have been considered a slum, as it was in Bangkok, but Tao Poon was a center of considerable wealth, illegal wealth. It wasn't about drugs, though drugs were available on a modest scale. It was all about gambling. Tao Poon was the impenetrable, for the police, gambling center of Bangkok. No police were allowed. All police payoffs were made outside of the Tao Poon zone and the police liked it that way. They couldn't be held accountable for what they didn't see.

Hell, Matt thought, let's go where the cops can't go.

Two heavily muscled goons were waiting at the double doored entrance to the gambling building. They were dressed in black jeans and black muscle shirts showing both their muscle and their oversized stomachs. Both were wearing several gold chains and good fortune amulets, somehow a common trait amongst Bangkok hoods.

"I'm here to meet Khun Jack." They nodded, opened one of the doors and waved him inside where he found another wary muscle object. "I'm here to meet Khun Jack."

He wouldn't be here without an invitation. It was an outlaw scene. As an outsider he would be inviting trouble. Jack was highly placed in the underworld gambling hierarchy of Bangkok. He apparently was hiding out here. If Jack was in danger of some sort there was no better place to hide out. No one could get into Tao Poon who wasn't connected or a known patron of the tables. Jack would be safe here but the question was, safe from what?

The interior had an opening hallway with a ceiling three floors up and double walkways flanking the entrance to another set of doors to the main gambling room straight ahead. Once again there was no talk. He was waved towards the staircase on the right leading to a second-floor hallway. Entering the hallway, he saw a series of doors on his left facing the interior of the building. The corridor walls seemed made of a dark wood, or was it years of smoke residue? There were lighting posts built down the hallway just above head level which provided weak circles of light as he moved ahead. At the middle of the hallway stood two more goons standing in front of a doorway. Matt recognized them as two of Jack's personal crew. Matt thought, there is no shortage of muscle here. For sure nobody has a chance to walk out on their losses.

He was waved through the door.

Jack was alone at the back of the room, seated at a round card table. He had his head in his hands and looked depressed. He had a deck of cards and his mobile phone lying on the table next to him. As Matt entered Jack gave him a weak smile but it was only his lips not his eyes. Jack was a vain man in his early fifties. He was a quite plump, soft and mild appearing figure with thinning, slicked down, black hair. He was wearing black dress slacks and a tailored light blue long-sleeved shirt with gold cuff links. Jack had started life as a tailor to make his mom happy and was always a sharp dresser. Normally he was also known for his quick smile and jokes but not today. He had a cup of coffee from which he took a quick sip before speaking to Matt.

"Khun Matt, thanks for coming so quickly. We...I have a problem...I need to discuss with you." He pointed to a chair across the table from him. "Please sit."

The use of the word 'we' got Matt's attention but he let it go for now.

"I'll speak straight. You know I have a daughter in college?"

Matt nodded.

"She's disappeared. I think she was kidnapped. Her mother is going crazy and blames me because of my business interests. When it first happened, I thought maybe it was the police mafia looking to kidnap me. That's why I came to hide here. But now I'm desperate to find her Khun Matt. I need you to help me. Help save my daughter."

Matt knew Jack's daughter was young, beautiful and spoiled. She had been playing at going to college for several years but word was she spent more time at nightclubs.

"Okay, Jack, slow down. First I'm not sure I'm the guy you should be talking to. Are you sure she didn't run off with one of those foreign models she likes so much?"

"I'm sure. I did send people to check at some of the scenes she favors. They were told a story...a drunken girl being carried out of a club by a couple of Thai men. Put into a car. That happened the night she didn't come home."

"When was this?"

"A week ago. We haven't heard a thing since."

"A week! Jack, why did you wait so long to ask for help?

Did you go to the police?"

Jack twisted his head to the side and looked at Matt with a scornful glance.

"I didn't wait. I started someone asking around immediately, but not the police. I was expecting a ransom demand for one thing. You know it could have been the police who kidnapped her. But of course they would have demanded money quickly."

"How can you be sure the girl at the club was your daughter?"

"Oi had a special girlfriend who was her partner in going to the clubs. I sent someone to talk with her and she admitted going to that club that night. She said she had gone to the bathroom to take some drugs and passed out. When the club staff woke her up later she was angry. She thought Oi had gone home with a friend and just left her."

"So she didn't see Oi leave?"

"No. What the doormen at the club said was that one girl, who had too much to drink, was walked out by two Thai guys dressed in black suits. They put her in a car and drove off together."

"Did the doormen have any idea who the guys were?"

"No just the opposite. The doormen said they had never seen these guys. They also said the guys looked *mai-di*, no good. They were big, very dark skinned and completely shaven. Not just their heads and faces but their eyebrows too, like monks. The doormen admitted they were scared of the two men."

"If she was kidnapped what are they after? Have you had a demand for money?"

"No. That's just it. There has been nothing. I would be happy to pay if it's money, I can handle that, but there's been nothing so far and it's a week now."

"You said no ransom demand was one reason you waited until now to contact me. Was there another reason?"

Jack leaned forward, hands rising from the table opening to Matt in almost a begging motion. Obviously they had gotten to an important aspect of the talk.

"Well that's why I said 'we' have a problem. I'm sorry, I did think of you right away but then I thought a more experienced, older, man would be better as I expected a negotiation for my daughter."

"So?"

"So I got in touch with your friend, the former American special forces soldier, Khun John Scales. He is known as one who negotiates between senior generals and, at times between senior generals and police and politicians who might have ties to my world. He has a good reputation in that regard. I thought he would ensure a reasonable agreement to get my daughter home."

Matt knew that by using the phrase 'my world' Jack meant the crime world; drugs, gambling, smuggling, loan sharking, et al., but he wanted to avoid saying that directly.

"I'm not offended. John is an excellent choice. He has the experience. He knows people and places I have no idea about. He is still physically capable of handling himself. I'm sure he'll be able to handle this for you. Why do you need me?"

"The problem Khun Matt is that when John and I talked a week ago he said the first thing he had to do was find out who these people were. He said he had to know who he was going to negotiate with in order to understand their motivations and to find their price. He asked me to give him four or five days to check around and then he would get back to me, sooner if possible."

"And?"

"Four or five days passed and then two days more. I have been trying his phone but there is no signal. I got worried and called the law office...the one he uses as a base for his special projects. They say they haven't seen him or heard from him since the day I first called and met with him. They have no idea where he is. This has never happened before. No matter where he is in the world and what project he is working on he always calls in every couple of days. They have had no contact and they are worried also."

"Oh shit."

"Yeah. Oh shit. What can we do? There is nobody better than Khun John. We have to find him or I'm afraid we'll never find my daughter. What can we do?"

"Okay. You got my attention. Let me follow up on whatever trail John might have gone down looking for your daughter."

CHAPTER FOUR

As he walked slowly back out of the gambling hall Matt no longer registered the details he had looked for on his way in. Then his mind was open, curious, taking in his surroundings. Now his mental focus was on the mission. Find Jack.

The guards opened the doors for him. As he walked down the alleyway his mind was on Jack and how to track him down. Walking in a fog of concentration, he didn't move quickly enough and was brushed by a motorbike whose driver yelled an insult at him but kept going. Okay, Matt thought, time to wake up. I need to talk to some people who can help.

He was sweating through his shirt as he arrived at the street scene at the end of the alleyway. It was the normal motorbike, taxi, passenger car, Bangkok traffic chaos. He threw his hand up, and a taxi cut across to the inside lane to pick him up at the curb. A motorbike rider that had been cut off yelled an insult at the driver and then wheeled around the taxi and took off again.

Matt leaned back against the seat and enjoyed the air-conditioned coolness inside the taxi. The taxi driver wasn't about to allow relaxation time in the taxi. He didn't turn to face Matt he just shouted into the windshield, "Where to?"

"Terminal 21" Matt replied. It was a well-known central Bangkok shopping landmark, and convenient, as it was across the street from Hustlers' pool hall. Hustlers served as his alternative office. It would be cool and quiet and a good place to ask

15

himself some questions.

After a few seconds, he took out his phone and called his girlfriend Noi. She knew and liked John and had always been a good foil for Matt. A talk with her would help him focus and plan. She was immediately responsive and agreed to meet him at Hustlers.

The ride through the streets and the highrise forest of downtown Bangkok was the usual chaos of stopping and starting, the taxi driver trying to find innovative ways of edging through the streets, missing red lights, trying to avoid street vendors and their carts, turning down small side streets off the main streets and returning again, time after time.

John was a best friend and mentor for Matt. They had met soon after Matt returned to Bangkok, after leaving the Rangers and resigning from military service. Matt had found immediately that he and John connected on many levels. Number one was that John had been a special ops warrior many years before and he still carried that psyche hidden within his low-key manner. Matt understood and admired that. They shared a bond growing out of the brotherhood of war. When Matt needed advice he went to John and John had never failed him. He strongly felt he couldn't fail John now.

After the taxi dropped him at Terminal 21, Matt took the stairs up to the crosswalk and over to the opposite sidewalk a few doors down from Hustlers. He heard some angry shouts and a woman screaming. As he looked ahead he saw it was one the attendants, Apple, who worked at the pool hall. She was backed up to the wall of the building and being beaten by a heavy-set man just outside the entrance to Hustlers. Matt broke into a run. As he neared the scene he didn't slow down to ask questions. The man was so intent on slapping Apple around that he didn't notice Matt until the last second and started to turn. Matt didn't hesitate but immediately threw a punch just below the man's ribcage.

The punch was effective. The man groaned and sagged to his

knees. As he fell Apple broke through his arms and ran through the door to the pool hall where two other attendants were gathered watching.

From his knees the man looked up at Matt. He had pitted facial skin and long black hair held back in a ponytail. He didn't want more, he held his hands up to Matt to show he was through and turned and tottered down the street.

Matt went into Hustlers. Apple was being looked after by the other attendants, but the bar itself was virtually empty in the early afternoon hours. Apple's face was red, showing the handprints where she had been slapped and her nose was bleeding. The girls gave her a towel to hold to her nose.

One of the girls looked up at Matt and said "It's okay Khun Matt. We'll take care of her now." The girls tried to lead Apple towards the back of the room towards the woman's toilet. Apple wouldn't go. She was still sobbing but seemed to be getting control of herself.

She shook the girls away and went to Matt grabbing his hands in hers.

"Khun Matt, thank you, thank you. I'm so embarrassed, please forgive me, but I need your help."

Matt felt the situation slipping out of control but he couldn't say no to Apple. He had known her for a long time. She was a 'good' girl as the Thai would say. She was a hard worker at the pool hall, cleaning the tables, racking the balls and occasionally shooting games with customers who had come in alone. She was not a sex worker or ever involved in anything shady. She was in her late twenties, without a husband and had a baby boy being cared for by her mother in a farming community located in the northern area known as Isan.

"Okay Apple." Matt nodded and showed her to the table he was going to sit at. It was a quiet spot out of the traffic lanes of the pool hall.

As they went, Apple turned to the other girls and signaled them to leave her and Matt alone. Her problems wouldn't be private for long but she wanted her talk with Matt to be private.

Matt sat at the table and motioned Apple to sit across from him. He had enough on his mind already without adding more to it, but Apple was a longtime friend and he couldn't ignore her problem.

"Apple, what's going on?"

Apple heaved a sigh and seemed to calm herself a bit more. "It's about money Khun Matt. My mom is sick and in the hospital. I needed to send the hospital money so they would take care of my mom. I was desperate and made a big mistake. I went to a loan man. He gave me money and told me I had to repay in a month. I knew I couldn't pay him myself but I thought I would be able to get my friends to help me and then repay them later, but nobody could." She put her head down on the table, not crying but seemingly unable to face Matt.

Matt understood. Loan sharking is big in Bangkok. The loan sharks are predators and once you take their money, it's difficult to escape. Oftentimes the cost was ten percent a week. It could be more depending on how desperate the person was. If a woman owed too much money to repay they would force her into prostitution. If a man could not repay they would take his wife and prostitute her. At the same time Matt thought what Apple needed now was a dose of hope.

"It's okay Apple. I'm sure there is a way out of this. We can find it. You just keep doing your job. I'll talk with some friends. Okay?"

Apple looked up, still shaken but with a small light of hope in her eyes. She put her hands together in a wai, the prayerful gesture the Thai use to show respect, nodding her head.

"Thank you Khun Matt. I have no other hope."

Matt showed no concern on his face but winced inwardly, being the only hope was not what he was looking for. "Apple, stay with one of your girlfriends for a while. Don't be alone when you come to work or go home. Understand?"

"Yes Khun Matt."

Apple got up from the table and went back to the other attendants who had been watching from the bar. They came up and gave her a hug. The girls would stick together.

Matt sat back with his head swimming. He had problems to address and he needed help sorting through them. Where was Noi?

CHAPTER FIVE

As he waited, one of the girls came over and brought Matt a soft drink. The girl attendants at Hustlers were not exotic in their dress, rather the uniform was a sports polo shirt with the pool hall's name on it and then black slacks or jean shorts. No makeup. The girls didn't want pool players confusing them with the legion of sex workers thronging the bars and central streets at night. To Matt they were all sisters. It was a comfortable relationship.

He was just catching his breath and trying to absorb the situation, now two situations he was involved in, when Noi came through the doors. He waved her over and sat back and relaxed a bit.

"Hey, thanks for coming. I have some things I need to talk out a bit with you."

Noi, in her early thirties, was five feet ten inches tall, very tall for a Thai girl. She had an athletic look, with her long black hair tied back. She was lean in build but not skinny. She was dressed, as she usually was during the day, in office casual, black dress slacks, low heels and a white no collar shirt with the sleeves partially rolled up. She wore no makeup and her only jewelry was a ring Matt had given her the year before. She had her own software company and, unusual for many Thai girls from middle or upper-class families, lived on her own, not with her parents. They had met several years back when Matt was helping out as an instructor on a rock-climbing course in the southern resort island of Phuket. They had been a couple ever since, though still living apart.

Noi had been smiling when she came in but as she saw the look of concern on Matt's face she adjusted to his vibe.

"Hey. What's up? You sounded pretty worried over the phone."

"Yeah, I'm really glad to see you. Thanks for getting away from the office for a while. Couple of problems I want to run by you."

"It's okay. We aren't too busy today. My staff is happy to attend to their bits and bytes without me looking over their shoulders."

Matt waved to one of the attendants to get a drink for Noi.

As the girl left the table, Matt turned back to Noi. Matt briefed her quickly on what had just transpired with Apple and the loan shark. Noi was shocked, public violence was unusual in Bangkok.

"What are you going to do?"

Matt looked at the pool girls watching them talk and shook his head, "Nothing now. I just told her I would try to help but she should not be alone and if possible stay with a girlfriend for now. I'll talk with Jack and ask him for a connection that can provide me some advice. He knows the gambling and loan shark world."

"Okay."

"I have a much bigger problem. Apparently John Scales has gone missing. I have to find him."

"What happened?"

"Jack asked me to meet him this morning. It seems his daughter was kidnapped out of a night club a week ago."

"So he wants you to help find her?"

"Not that simple. He asked John Scales for help first. John agreed and told Jack he would report back in a couple of days. It's been a week now and no word from John. So we have two people missing. Jack wants his daughter back but feels if I can track down John Scales it will lead to his daughter. Needless to say he is somewhat desperate."

"Has he been asked for money?"

"No and that's the second strange thing in addition to John's disappearance. There's been no request for money. There are kidnappings in Bangkok but they always ask for money. This is something out of the norm."

Noi didn't care much for Jack, but John Scales was different. She had respected and liked him immediately on meeting him. He spoke very polite Thai and, despite his military bearing and background, projected a fatherly image that appealed to her.

"What are you going to do first?"

"Well, I have two points of contact. The first is the nightclub. I'll go over there early tonight before it gets busy and talk with the doormen. There might be something more there. The other stop will have to be Lek, Oi's girlfriend and night clubbing buddy."

"You can handle the guys at the nightclub but how about the girl? Want me to help with that?"

Matt paused; he had asked Noi for research help on cases before but this would be a new step, direct involvement with someone involved in the case. At the same time, it seemed obvious that a woman's touch would be less threatening and probably more productive than his.

"Okay. If you have time, see if you can meet with her early tomorrow. Meet outside of her home if possible. Take her for coffee. She will probably be more open if it's just you two."

"Anything specific you want me to ask her?"

"I find it hard to think these guys walked in and took a girl out of a night club without looking over the scene and other possible scenarios the girls frequented. Have her walk through her last month's outings. See if there are any unusual incidents or people that she can remember. There must be something there if she can focus and remember it."

"Okay. Anything else? Why don't I do a search on any news the past six months on unusual night club incidents and anything related to kidnappings, attempted kidnappings or missing girls?"

"Yeah. That would be helpful. Maybe this is not a one off. Maybe there is a kidnap scheme going on that hasn't become public."

"You don't want to go to Neung with this?"

Neung was one of Matt's closest Thai friends. He had gone through the U.S. Army Ranger school with Matt years before. He was now a senior officer in the Thai Department of Special Investigation, akin to the U.S. FBI. They had worked together on previous cases and he was the best guide Matt had to the labyrinth that was the Thai national police bureaucracy.

"No, at least not now. Jack is trying to keep this out of official police hands and I have to respect his wishes, at least for the moment. I might have to go to Neung unofficially if we can't get the leads we need on our own."

"Okay Matt, but one thing. At some point you are going to need some backup. John would have been the logical one. Since he's not here, promise me you'll think about someone reliable who can help you on this. Don't go it alone."

Matt smiled, he wasn't used to having a caretaker but it was nice coming from Noi. "Okay babe. You go back to work. I'm going to go work out and think things over before going over to the nightclub later. Let's talk and compare notes tomorrow."

CHAPTER SIX

John Scales sat at his observation point on the jungle hill over-looking the valley. Looking down from the hilltop the valley looked much like any farming valley in Southern Thailand. There were rice paddies, dotted with coconut palms, stretching the full length of the valley. The rice stalks, tall and waving in the breeze, were ready for harvest. There was a small village, a cluster of thatched roof huts, gathered at the mouth of the valley along the dirt road that ran down the center.

He was covered with sweat. His hair was matted with drops periodically sliding down his forehead and into his eyes. He would slowly reach up, remove his bush hat and use a dark towel he always carried to mop up the moisture before slowly replacing the hat. Controlling movement was the essence of remaining hidden, no movement was best but definitely no quick movements could be made. At least, John thought, he had shade from the tree he was lying under and wasn't exposed to the sun.

Occasionally a slight breeze stirred. He was wearing cam-ouflage clothing and his old U.S. army cloth field hat. He was confident that as long as he stayed in the shadows of the trees and didn't move too much he wouldn't be noticed by those down in the valley. There was a steady chirping of birds and he was mindful that he couldn't frighten them and have the flock fly out en masse and draw attention to his site. He had stayed under cover since the previous day observing activity in the temple complex. His contact in the Border Patrol Police had been proven right. This was the temple that didn't exist. A temple apart from the official sangha order.

It was much more than an ordinary temple layout, however. It could possibly be called a temple complex as there was a large central temple building but of an unusual construction. It looked more like a giant flying saucer, a gold-colored flying saucer topped by a dome which he guessed would be termed a stupa in a more normal Buddhist religious setting. The temple grounds were surrounded by a cinder block wall, possibly nine feet in height. Inside the wall there were also a multitude of side buildings, some were the conventional kutis in which monks resided, the crematorium building, and some sheds to shelter vehicles. The overall impression was of an almost military style order. In fact, as he watched he noticed two-man teams of guards dressed in black uniforms, carrying automatic rifles, coming out periodically to walk around the perimeter while scanning the wood line.

Why was this a secret? What was it about this temple, the monks within, and their activities that was the basis for such secrecy and security? His contact had told him there had been rumors of young girls sighted in cars going this way through the back roads. The contact also said there were rumors the monks of this temple, and by extension this sect, might have answers about the missing girl. He certainly wasn't going to get the answers by walking up and knocking on the door.

He checked his phone again. No signal. The location was too far into the jungle and mountains for any company to put up a tower. Looking back at the temple dome though he saw what looked to be a signal dish and a black antenna poking up. They obviously had full communications with the outside world.

As he scanned the valley with his binoculars a black car drove up the dirt road towards the temple's main entrance, stirring a cloud of dust into the air. There were two guards at the entrance, not police but outfitted like police. As the car slowed and drove through the entrance both men bowed their heads and gave a deep wai to whomever was the passenger in the car.

Inside the temple grounds the car stopped. A man wearing a black suit got out of the front seat and bowing his head opened the back door. A short, somewhat wizened man, dressed in a monk's saffron robes, got out of the car and walked towards the entrance to the main temple building. On the steps leading into the temple, six more men dressed as monks had appeared. They also bowed their heads and each gave a deep wai, hands clasped to their face in a prayer gesture, to the arriving monk. He dipped his head in acknowledgment and walked through the entrance. They followed him inside. The man in the suit got back into the car and drove it around and parked next to another car and three pick-up trucks parked in back of the temple.

John had been taking pictures since the car arrived. He put the camera down, leaned back and thought. Good, that little monk must be part of the answer. They certainly treat him as if he is the next thing to the Buddha. Just who the hell is he? Why is he here?

It had taken him three days of rough going circling through a maze of remote dirt roads on his motorbike and then hiking through the jungle to get here. He had found all he could on this visit. There was no sense alerting their security that the temple was of interest. They had tucked it as far back in the mountains and jungle close to the border with Malaysia as possible to keep it hidden. Let them think it was still hidden.

After dark he moved back through the jungle, back up the mountainside. He would camp on the reverse slope, away from the temple, tonight. Tomorrow he would push back to his hidden motorbike and make his way out. He needed more information and a whole lot of backup if he was to take this further.

CHAPTER SEVEN

A workout always cleared Matt's head when hard thinking was needed. The interior of the old gym was not well lit even with some sunshine coming through the row of windows high on the walls just under the ceilings. The windows were open. The large standing fans, scattered around the floor, worked hard, but failed, in an attempt to blow the sour aroma of the workouts out of the gym. The centerpiece of the gym was the Muay Thai boxing ring standing three feet off the ground, the altar of the establishment.

Off to one side of the gym, one of the heavy bags moved with the force of the hits. It was the constant opponent, always coming back into place. Matt hit it, circled, kicked it and hit it again. The sweat bounced off him with each bit of violence. It was a workout not just of muscle but of muscle memory and technique. For Matt it was more than science though, it was also emotion. A release for whatever frustrations or problems bothered him. Each blow was delivered with a loud grunt, he was punishing the bag, destroying his problems. The volume of his grunts and the whack of the destructive blows on the bag grew as he entered his personal zone of destruction. Finally, as he tapered down he stopped the bag and looked around.

The others working out in the gym and the two young boxers in the ring had all stopped and were staring at Matt. Normally his workout was ignored. He was just part of a familiar family scene. It was a close knit Muay Thai boxing community. Today however he had brought an unaccustomed aggression to the scene. Matt was embarrassed and nodded his head slightly to indicate all was good.

Coach Somchai, the owner of the gym, was working in the ring with the apprentice boxers. The coach, a mentor and friend for Matt, was a past Muay Thai champion of Thailand. The two fourteen-year-old boxers were street kids from a group the coach had taken under his wing. Early on his return to Bangkok, Matt had met the coach, who had introduced him to the martial art form of Muay Thai. The coach encouraged Matt's growing ability and dedication to the Muay Thai world. He was looking at Matt now with a bit of concern but nodded back when Matt nodded to him and the rest of the gym rats. It would be okay.

The world outside, any problems he might have, were always lost to Matt in the rhythm of his workouts. He resumed circling the heavy bag, kicking at different levels, hitting mid-body targets. The frustration was gone. He felt more relaxed now.

Somehow the unconscious mind is always at work. As the workout finished Matt had some thoughts about how to proceed. He would take some time and go back to Hustler's and meet with Apple again. As he cooled down and toweled off, Matt decided to call Jack for advice on helping Apple with the loan shark. Jack had asked him for a favor, he would ask Jack for a favor.

Jack answered on the first ring.

"Hi Matt, my daughter?"

"No Jack. Not yet. I'll be talking to some people tonight. I want to ask you for a contact. Someone who would know something about the loan shark operation in the area of your bar and Hustlers."

"What are you after?"

"One of the girls at Hustlers was beaten up by one of the gang for overdue money. I want to see if I can help her out in some way."

"Hey, I don't do that business."

"Yeah Jack, I know, but you still know a lot of people don't you?"

Jack paused for a minute and then said, "Okay. I think you can talk with Police Sergeant Sombat from the Lumpini Station. He's a friend of my bar. I know he doesn't like those loan people. I'll give him a call and he will contact you."

"Okay Jack. Thanks. I'll be back to you with anything about Oi."

Matt was relieved. He had met Sgt. Sombat before when the police officer was on his rounds collecting protection money from the bars for the Lumpini station. Sgt. Sombat had been friendly. He knew the area well. It would be a good place to start.

The scene at Hustlers had changed dramatically. The pool bar was now busy with the early evening crowd. All the tables had players shooting and the click of the balls was softly cascading throughout the hall. Rock was playing over the speakers, nothing too heavy or too loud, the players were all about focusing on their shots. The dress was mostly T-shirts or polo shirts and jeans, nothing upmarket. The pool girls were hustling to keep up with the action, closely monitoring the needs of the men at the tables. It was an international mix, Brits, Europeans, Americans, Japanese, Filipinos and Thai. The Japanese only shot pool with other Japanese just taking one of the tables while the rest watched and commented. A group of players sat at the bar or on chairs around the entrance way, some betting on games they watched, others just waiting their chance at the right opponent.

Matt caught Apple's eye and she pointed at some tables outside the bar where they could sit and talk with relative privacy for a few minutes.

Apple was clearly nervous as she sat at the table across from Matt. Before Matt could talk about the advice he had received— that he should talk with Sgt. Sombat—she held up a hand to signal him not to talk.

"Khun Matt I've been thinking about this. I don't want

trouble. I shouldn't have borrowed the money but now I think I have to pay or do whatever they are asking. I can't give the money back now but they said I could work it off."

She was trembling as she spoke and Matt could see she was clearly afraid. Something had happened. The light in the sitting area outside the bar was dim but as he looked closely he could see the bruises on her face from the beating she had taken.

"Apple is your mom still in the hospital?"

"Yes Khun Matt. Her kidneys are failing. The doctor says that's why the treatments are so expensive."

"So whatever you do for these guys you still won't have money to pay the hospital bills will you?"

"No Khun Matt but I have no choice. These guys came here. They made noise. If this happens again I could lose my job."

"When did they say to meet next?"

Now Apple was crying, "They gave me five days. If I don't have the money paid in full by then, plus another ten thousand baht, they will go to the hospital and visit my mom. I can't let that happen Khun Matt."

"Okay, we'll fix this. I'll talk to some friends. When the time for the five days meeting comes let's talk first. I will make sure the money is available. One way or another we will finish this. Okay?"

"You can do this?"

"We can do this. For now, do nothing. Let me know if they call you again and ask for a meeting earlier. Don't go to meet them without me or letting me and my friends make arrangements okay?"

When Matt left Apple it was with real anger. There was no protection at the bottom of the Bangkok income scale, the system fed on the poor. He hoped he could deliver on his promise. He hoped Sgt. Sombat's show of respect for him when they had met previously would translate into some real action to help Apple.

Now it was time to go see if the men at the nightclub had anything to add to the kidnapping story.

CHAPTER EIGHT

Responding to Jack's call to their manager, the two doormen who were at work the night Oi went missing had come in early. The place was quiet and the parking lot empty. It was much too early for the night crowd this place attracted. The cars busily passing on the adjacent street were late working office staff on their way home.

As Matt approached the two men it was obvious they were nervous. One of them was sitting in a chair looking off to the side. Clearly he didn't want to talk. At the same time, they had been ordered by their boss to talk with Matt. One man, over-weight, large and well-muscled, just stared at Matt.

Matt decided to go easy to start. He focused on the bigger of the two as he seemed ready to engage.

"You were on duty last week when a drunken girl was carried out?"

The man looked at Matt for a minute, seemingly reluctant to speak, and then nodded.

"We were here. We saw a girl leave. We told this to the men who came before."

Matt thought a mild threat wouldn't hurt.

"Yes. It's good you did, but we need to know more. You can help us can't you?"

The man sitting in the chair looked around at this. The use of 'we' had gotten his attention. Was Matt talking for the big bosses?

"What more?"

Matt smiled. The door had been opened.

"Details. You said there were three men. One man was driving the car. Two men went inside the club and brought the girl out. You described the two men and the car. What about the man in the car?"

That surprised the doormen. The large one looked to the man sitting in the chair who responded.

"He wouldn't get out of the car so I'm not sure what he looked like. He was dark skinned and wore a Muslim cap."

"Good. That's helpful. What about the car, big and black isn't much help. Was there anything else? Something special with this car. What about the license plates?"

The two men looked at each other, now clearly nervous Matt was pushing them more than Jack's men had. The man in the chair answered.

"They weren't Bangkok plates. We always look to see if someone has VIP plates. These were from down south I think, maybe Naratiwat."

"Did they say anything?"

"No. They came. Went right in and came out with the girl in five minutes. Otherwise we would have made the car move."

"Did the girl say anything?"

"No. She was too drunk. It happens. Every week some girl drinks too much and gets carried out."

He gave Matt a hard stare. It was clear that further answers would be no. It seemed they were scared of Jack's guys but somehow more scared of someone else.

Matt looked at them for a minute, then decided to leave it for now.

"Thanks. We may have to talk later."

The two men looked at each other. That was not a welcome comment.

As Matt walked away he decided on one more stop before calling it a night. He needed to check out John Scales apartment.

He would go and look around to see if there was anything there that might be helpful. Then he could exchange information with Noi in the morning following her visit with the girl, Lek, who had gone along to the nightclub that night.

John's apartment had a keypad allowing entry at the bottom level. Matt had the number from previous visits and walked through the lobby and took the elevator to the 7th floor. John had explained he didn't like to be too high up in buildings in case of fire, thus keeping to the lower floors.

John had secreted an extra key for emergencies and had once shown Matt where it was hidden, in a small box magnetically attached in back of the electric switch connections for the floor, in case a day like this should ever come. However, when Matt went to the box, the key wasn't there.

That got Matt's attention and stopped him. Had John lost a key? Had he changed the hiding place or just decided it was a bad idea to hide a key?

Matt went over to the door to John's apartment. It was closed but when he tried the handle it opened. Matt paused at the door, holding it only slightly open. There were no lights on inside and, as he listened, no sound.

John had once advised him that, when he was working on a case in which violence was involved, he should always be carrying his sidearm. Matt swore at himself for not following the rule. Maybe his excuse was that he had just gotten on to this case today. Maybe his excuse was that he couldn't at this point classify the case as one of violence. No matter Matt thought, he would have felt better if he had his gun with him.

Taking a breath, he eased open the door and entered the room slowly; conscious he was outlined in the hallway light behind him he stepped to the side. He slowly put the door back almost completely closed, took two steps into the room and waited for his eyes to adjust to the dark before looking for a light switch.

However, someone beat him to it.

The lights went on. The command came at the same time. "Freeze, right there, asshole. Don't move."

Matt froze and stared speechless at the source of the command. It was a woman. A woman with a gun pointed right at him. She was about five feet ten inches tall, wearing a black leather jacket and black jeans. He noted she was wearing similar hiking shoes to the ones he wore. Her black hair was swept back in a short ponytail. No makeup. No jewelry except for a ring on one hand holding a green jewel. She was Asian, possibly Thai, possibly Chinese, but the accent was straight American. The attitude was straight cop but from where he couldn't guess.

He found his voice, "Who are you? What are you doing here?"

This seemed to cause her some amusement, at least her eyes showed amusement. The rest of her face and posture with a two-handed grip on the gun, were carved from stone as was her response.

"Who am I? I'm the one with the gun asshole. Now, who are you and what are you doing here?"

Matt was pissed off, pissed off at himself for getting into this situation and pissed off at the girl with the gun and the attitude who was obviously, but carefully, enjoying his discomfort. She had him cold. He was too far into the room to turn back yet she was ten feet away with furniture in between them. Movement in any direction wouldn't work.

"My name is Matt Chance. I'm a friend of John's. I'm here checking on him okay? Now who the hell are you?"

"I'm still the one with the gun. Now answer another question and maybe we'll disarm a bit. Why are you checking on John? What's up?"

Matt was fuming now but losing his cool wouldn't improve the situation.

"I got called by some people who had hired John for a job. They say he's several days overdue to check in. They asked me to follow up and see if I could locate him and get the status on

the case he's working. That's why I'm here. Now who the hell are you and why are you here?"

Now she smiled, not a big smile, a tight one, but a smile nonetheless, she seemed to be enjoying herself. She put the gun away in a shoulder holster where it would be hidden by the light leather jacket she was wearing. She pointed at an easy chair near Matt and said, "Why don't you sit down Matt Chance and we'll have a talk."

Matt did as she directed but she kept her distance and continued standing. The smile however did broaden a bit. She had an athletic and lean build. Her facial features were attractive, with strong cheekbones and large almond eyes, with a wide mouth when she smiled but narrow lips. He would guess her age in the early thirties but there were no lines in her face. She was undoubtedly attractive but he wasn't feeling the attraction at the moment.

She didn't answer Matt's question but asked another one. "I take it John didn't tell you about me?"

"No. Should he have?"

"It's just that he said he would. He intended to introduce us. He thinks a lot of you. He respects your military service. He talked about the cases you've worked on with him since returning to Thailand a few years back. Truth be told, I think he looks on you as a son."

She paused to let Matt absorb that.

"So, who am I? My name is Jade Lee. My dad is Chinese. My mom was Thai. I grew up in America. My mom died a few years back when I was on duty in Afghanistan."

"You were military?"

"Don't interrupt. You'll get the full story or at least the full story I want you to have."

Jade continued. "Yeah. West Point 2007. I went army aviation, flying Black Hawks. Like you, at least according to John, I got tired of it and the self-serving promotion mania of the career military. I resigned and decided to come back to my mom's home country for a while, again, possibly not unlike you. That was a year ago." Shoulder shrug. "I'm still here."

Matt digested this and, as was happening so much lately, decided what was not being said was probably more important than what was being said. At the same time, he couldn't help poking her a bit.

"Are you sure you weren't a cop in the army?"

She laughed. "Really? It's my attitude showing again isn't it? I'll have to work on that. No, I was never a cop. I'm just a woman who believes in being prepared."

"How did you hook up with John?"

"He found me not too long after I got here. He had a job that required knowledge of choppers, including having someone who would back him up and who could fly one. My training includes a lot of work with handguns and martial arts. Some friends of mine in the Thai military found out what he was looking for and he called me. We hit it off and have done some work together since then."

Waving his hand at the apartment, Matt asked, "What brought you here?"

"I called the office of the law firm he occasionally works with to check on him. They usually know where he is and how to contact him. This time the secretary told me what I guess she told you, that she was worried. He was missing and people had called looking for him. Possibly you? Then I thought I had better start looking for his trail. This was the first place I thought to look. Now, tell me, what the hell is going on. Is John in trouble?"

This gun toting woman was not something in Matt's experience and he wasn't really comfortable with her, especially with the way she had amused herself by holding the gun on him way past the point she knew he wasn't a threat. However, John came first. If she could help he would work with her.

"I think so. Let me fill you in. We don't really know each other but maybe, with John as the connection, we can do something together."

Again the amused look. She just nodded and smiled, "Maybe we can."

CHAPTER NINE

The boats were coming into shore from the night's fishing. It had been a windy and somewhat rough night at sea. Fisherman Somchai and his thirty-year-old son Anut were running late and were the last to come in. The sun was breaking over the gulf of Thailand behind them as they steered their boat through the swells and towards the beach. The bamboo shack fifty meters up on the shore, underneath the swaying coconut palms, was their home.

Anut called out to his dad pointing at some rocks jutting out from the ocean near the shoreline. There were a couple of monitor lizards nosing around something hanging on the rocks. From a distance it looked like a collection of dirty white rags or sheets tumbled together by the waves and deposited on the rocks by the currents at high tide. However, when they got closer to shore they could see a hand hanging down towards the water. There was a body inside the white clothes. As they watched one of the monitor lizards, five feet in length, splashed towards the rock nosing at the hand. The lizards were not considered dangerous but they were carrion eaters. If there was something dead in their territory they would eat it.

As they beached their boat, the father called to other fisherman further up the shore asking them to help. They formed a group and went out into the waves towards the rocks. Several of the men and some older children who had followed were throwing stones at the lizards to scare them away.

When they reached the body, they could see that the lizards had already been tearing at it. The police report submitted later would use the indelicate phrase, 'partially devoured.' The main upper body and head were still intact. It was a girl. She was covered only by the dirty white robe. They tugged on the robe, not wanting to touch the body, wrapping the body in it as it slid off the rocks, and carried it back to shore.

When they laid the body out on the sand they could see that she was young, possibly barely out of her teens. Once she had been very beautiful but now her lifeless eyes and pale skin, devoid of color, frightened them all. The ghost of this girl would surely haunt this beach site now. They would have to move their village. How had she come to be here?

CHAPTER TEN

Before heading home Matt decided to make one final stop. He knew Police Sergeant Sombat from seeing him previously on his collection rounds at pool bars Matt played at. The police wore their brown uniforms and carried their sidearms when making their collection rounds. Of course Matt had never seen the envelopes passed, that was done discretely when no one was around except the bar manager after closing hours. Matt had seen Sombat at the bar however, having a free drink, engaging in friendly banter with the employees, but almost never with the bar's customers.

On one occasion Matt had politely nodded to the police sergeant. Sombat had nodded back, giving Matt a curious look. He then walked over to talk with Matt.

Sombat asked him, "You are the American?"

Matt nodded, yes he was.

"You are the ranger?"

Again Matt nodded yes, wondering where this was going.

Then the sergeant just gave him a thumbs up and a big smile, "Very good, very good," and walked back to his drink. Matt later found out the sergeant had served as a ranger in the Thai army before coming to the police force in Bangkok.

Matt knew that all of the Thai government offices were a mafia. The two biggest and most influential mafia were the army and the national police. In normal times they were like two roosters strutting around the farmyard. Not to be interfered with. Now however the army generals ruled the roost at the top government level. The police were still a major force however and the more visible graft, at the local level, was still theirs. No bar or even street vendor in a station's district would be exempt from monthly payment.

Matt phoned a couple of pool bars and found out Sombat was expected soon on his rounds at Spanky's bar on Sukhumvit Soi 15. He went over to the bar and camped at a table waiting. When Sombat came in Matt waited until the sergeant had seated himself comfortably at the bar and had a chance to chat with the bartender and the manager. When the manager went to the other end of the bar Matt went to her first, as a courtesy, and mentioned he would like to have a private conversation with the police sergeant. The manager just shrugged her shoulders, okay.

Sombat smiled as Matt approached which was a good sign.

Matt gave him a respectful wai in greeting. Sombat returned the gesture, which was also a good sign. Most times the police would barely deign to nod to foreigners. Sombat obviously viewed Matt differently, somehow as one who should be treated with normal respect.

"How are you doing Sergeant? I hope all is well."

"I'm very good Khun Matt, what can I do for you?"

Matt described Apple's problem and asked Sombat for his advice.

Sgt. Sombat gave a sigh.

"I'm sorry to hear that Khun Matt. Khun Apple is a good girl. I'm sorry to hear about her problem."

Sgt. Sombat leaned back in his chair. Matt felt he could see the wheels turning in the police sergeant's head as he pondered who might be behind this loan shark and what possible high connections the person might have. It was important for his self-protection to know how high the protection went for the loan shark.

"Listen Khun Matt my station doesn't want these people,

these loan sharks, doing their business here in our district. I appreciate your calling this to my attention. Let me ask some questions around the station. I'll get back to you soon."

"Thanks sergeant. They only gave her a few days. I don't want to see her beat up again."

"Soon, Khun Matt, soon. We'll talk again. Oh, Khun Matt, also you have to know, it will do no good to just remove the man who is bothering her. They will have records of debts owed and someone will just come in his place. We will need to get all the snakes in that den at one time."

"Okay, thanks sergeant. I'll wait to hear from you."

CHAPTER ELEVEN

It had stopped raining, but the trees were still dripping from the rain during the night. The ground underfoot was soaked and mud slick with small pools of water. John was exhausted as he moved back through the jungle. I should have found a way to get the motorbike closer. I've overdone it with this trip, he thought. I'm getting too old for this stuff.

He wanted to move through the jungle quickly, but his years of experience slipping through jungle settings in combat in several south-east Asian countries had inculcated in him a strong sense of the need to maintain noise discipline. Security always came first whether there was a known immediate threat or not.

Going back out on the same trail always seemed the easier way to return. John however stuck to habit, gained in his years on patrol, of never going back the way you came out. It was nearing night as he approached the vicinity where he had hidden the motorbike. Then, sniffing the air, he picked up the scent. There was cigarette smoke on the breeze. Not just cigarette smoke but the pungent clove type favored in parts of Thailand, Malaysia and Indonesia. He had company, very probably his motorbike had been found and they were waiting for him to come back to it.

The questions were, who was tracking him and how many? He took it for granted they were armed.

John had been in this corner of Thailand before. This was

the territory of Thailand's separatist Islamic insurgents, virtually a separate state in some areas.

It was time to slow down the world. He wouldn't be going anywhere tonight, possibly ever if he made a mistake now. He backed slowly up the faint animal trail he had been tracking down, looking for cover, a clump of bushes or a rock ledge he could hunker behind and still observe down the hillside to the dirt road he had taken to come in.

He needed to take stock. He was low on food and water as he hadn't expected to be out more than three days and this was the fifth day coming to a close. He was armed. He had his Sig Sauer 226 and five clips but there could be little doubt that the men below him were armed with automatic rifles. They probably carried M-16s and M-4s they had stolen from Thai army inventories or taken from the bodies of soldiers after ambushes. Getting into a shootout was not the answer.

The good news was that they didn't seem to know he was in their immediate area. They were waiting for him, not searching. He could hear occasional loud voices from below and now he could see the glow of a fire as they prepared to cook dinner and spend the night. He couldn't be sure of what they were saying as they were speaking the local Pattani dialect which was much closer to Malay than Thai. For now, he would observe.

He decided to pull back a bit more, take a nap and wait for night. Then, when they were sleeping, he would scout around their position. There was no way he could walk all the way back out to the ocean-side highway safely, but possibly an alternative would present itself. Let them eat and go to sleep for the night. Then he would look around.

CHAPTER TWELVE

The morgue in Naratiwat was a simple facility lacking the equipment she had at hand in Bangkok. However, Khun Wannee, a senior government pathologist and forensics specialist, had been told by the military authorities that the autopsy procedures she had been invited to perform on the yet unidentified girl would have to be done in the southern city. She had no choice but to comply. She relaxed her shoulders and reached for a scalpel from the equipment tray next to the autopsy table. 'Invitations' from the representatives of the military junta couldn't be turned down. So here she was, trying to do her best with limited tools. She had tried to get them to accept that one of the usual police medical examiners could do the job but the military made it clear it wasn't a job for the police. Why the politics of the situation went this way she wasn't sure but she was sure it was in her interest to comply.

Khun Wannee was left alone to undertake the procedure. As she always did, she talked to the victim. She had originally intended to practice medicine but in school had been drawn to the scientific analysis side of forensic medicine. At the same time, as a devout Buddhist, she felt her work was an important step in preparing her patients, as she thought of them, for the religious rituals that would send them to the next life.

Noting the bite marks and sections of the limbs that had been chewed on by the monitor lizards, she was moved to talk now. "You are such a pretty young lady and you've been treated so badly. Don't worry daughter, I will treat you as kindly and carefully as I can. You'll be clean and cared for as you go to the next life."

As she went through her procedures she could see that the girl, probably in her early twenties, had died by drowning, that was clear though the body had not been in the water long. It was probably just dumped into the water the night before it washed up on the rocks. It was also clear that it was most probably murder. She had severe bruising on her arms, back and neck and indications of repeated sexual assault. She had drugs in her system including ketamine, a drug that induced compliance and was probably responsible for the loss of consciousness that made it easier for her killers to take her body out to sea and dump it that night.

Identifying marks on the body were few though the girl had a tattoo that was quite unusual for a Buddhist nun, or bhikkhuni, if indeed that's what she was. Below her waistline, on her right groin, there was a tattoo of a small devil figure smiling and holding a spear pointed down towards her pubic region.

Wannee smiled kindly, "Well daughter, at some point in your life you definitely had a sense of sexual adventure. Is that what brought you here?"

Wannee paused and contemplated her patient. Many times she felt that, if she gave them time, her patients spoke to her. Not in words but in impressions or thoughts that occurred as she slowed herself and the forensic process down.

Now, contemplating the tattoo she could feel that this wasn't a poor country girl. At least she didn't have any of the Sak Yant or Thai temple tattoos that many country girls carried on their backs. Conclusion, probably a city girl, certainly not Muslim or from the deep south.

Then the questions were, what was she doing hair shaved

and in a nun's garb, this far south? Who or what organization was sponsoring her or had brought her to this site? Who had killed her? Why? And of course the biggest question was, who was she? Answering that would probably give the answers to the other questions. Apart from the tattoo there was nothing to help identify the girl.

Answering all those questions was not her job. Actually the senior army officer who had accompanied her on the helicopter ride to Naratiwat did not raise any of those issues except for looking for answers to the usual causes of death questions and the big one, things which might help to identify the girl. She suspected they had some of the answers but they were clearly not interested in sharing with her. So be it. She would summarize her information, give it to them and go back home accepting their very strong warning not to mention the case to anyone.

She had only asked one question and not gotten a satisfactory answer to it. "Would the girl be given a full Buddhist funeral and cremation so her spirit could be released to the next life?" When the army colonel who had taken her down to Naratiwat paused, she could see they hadn't even thought about that. That failure to consider the spiritual side of the matter bothered her greatly. She said nothing, but took that dissatisfaction back to Bangkok with her.

CHAPTER THIRTEEN

Matt had arranged to meet and exchange information with Noi. Jade was to be included and, considering Jade's somewhat standout presence, he felt they needed a discreet place. But where to meet? It had to offer more cover than a hotel coffee shop.

The answer came as he was thinking about the fact that he was constrained on calling in favors from the police and his other usual contacts by the fact that virtually no one knew of the kidnapping and Jack wanted it kept quiet for now. Then it hit him, Jack was hiding out at the Tao Poon casino, his pool bar was still available. Jack's Pool Bar didn't open until 1 p.m. so it would be deserted except for the handful of staff who slept up on the second floor. He called Jack and arranged to have the doors opened, the air conditioning on and coffee and tea available at 11 a.m.

The pool bar site was a bit out of Noi's way during the day but she didn't complain. She had met Matt there many times after work and could find her way. When he called Jade she didn't want directions, she just asked for a nearby reference point for Google maps, in this case Matt cited the Asoke BTS stop just up the alley way from the pool bar. When he asked where she would be coming from she just deflected the question.

Matt got there early to insure it would be open when Noi and Jade arrived. Noi arrived first which was good as he wanted time to broach the subject of Jade's inclusion in the meeting and the search for John. Matt had told Jade the meeting was at 11:30 a.m. to insure he had time to lay the groundwork with Noi.

Her response, when Matt said a female friend of Johns would be joining them and helping in the search, was predictable and possibly tinged by a hint of emerging jealousy.

"How do you know you can trust this woman? Even if she has a military background as you say, she's new here in Thailand and in any case she's just a girl."

It surprised Matt—this willingness of women to put one another down. The idea that there might be a bit of jealousy involved had not occurred to him. Of course, Matt had somehow neglected to mention to Noi that Jade had been holding him at gunpoint as they exchanged introductions the night before.

Matt gave her a wry smile, "Well as I told you she is not 'just a girl.' I trust John's judgment completely and if he thought she was good enough to work with, I think the same. In any case she is going to be looking for John also so we might as well at least share information."

As he spoke, a black and red Harley motorcycle roared up the alleyway into the courtyard area used as a car park by Jack's customers. The normal rumble of the chopper's engine was greatly amplified by the four-story high concrete walls of the narrow alleyway. All conversation stopped.

Jade, again dressed all in black and wearing the light leather jacket, parked, got off the bike, took off her helmet and shook her hair out. She looked around the buildings, older concrete block construction stained by mildew from the rain, and then the roofs for a second, before she turned and walked towards the door.

Matt thought, this is going to be interesting.

Noi was mesmerized. She turned back to Matt.

"This is the girl?"

"Yes, but as I said, she's not 'just a girl' Okay?"

Noi, somewhat recovering her composure, nodded but then said, "Okay, I can see that, but let's see what she says."

Matt smiled and turned in his chair and faced the door as Jade came in.

"Nice bike. Anyone in the neighborhood who thought they would sleep late today just had their plans changed."

Jade gave him a tight smile and had that amused look in her eyes that Matt had seen so much of the night before. It seemed she found amusement in most of the settings she encountered in life.

Jade's smile broadened as she walked over and stuck her hand out to Noi who was unsure whether to give her a formal wai in greeting or not. She accepted the handshake.

"Hi, I'm Jade. I guess Matt has told you I'm a friend of Johns and want to help find him."

Noi just nodded and there was an awkward pause as the two women eyed each other up and down, going through the normal five second female to female assessment that took in so much.

Assessment over, Jade took a seat at the table. Her jacket opened partially and Matt noted she was not carrying the gun she had brandished at him the night before.

"Sorry about the noise, these narrow alleys and high walls do reflect the bike's lovely rumble somewhat. What's up?"

Matt continued the introductions, giving Jade a little more background on how Noi's computer research had helped him in a couple of past cases. He didn't go into the depth of their relationship, though he had no doubt Jade would pick up on it as they talked.

Then Matt gave a report on his success, or lack of it, in questioning the doormen at the nightclub the previous evening. He mentioned the comment about the car's driver wearing a Muslim skull cap which, along with the license plates not being from Bangkok, raised the possibility that the kidnapping was organized in the south of Thailand.

He turned to Noi, "How did your meeting with the girlfriend go?"

"I was able to have private talk. She is still very upset, crying at times. She feels guilty she passed out in the lady's room. I asked her if the two of them had been aware of being stalked by guys who fit the description of the two men."

Here Noi laughed, a bit cynically and shook her head.

"What?"

"She said they had seen some very dark-skinned Thai guys standing on the edges of the crowd at several clubs but hadn't paid them any attention. She and her girlfriend were focused on the foreign boys. She said both their parents had warned them that coming from rich families they had to be careful of their friends. They had never thought of kidnapping."

Noi continued, "I did some research on press background or police statements about young Thai women disappearing or being injured at nightclubs. That pretty much came up blank. I found some reports of foreign girls getting stoned at full moon parties and then raped afterwards on the beach or in a nearby hut, but nothing on Thai girls that would seem to fit what we're looking for here."

Then she paused seemingly unsure of whether to say more. Matt prompted her.

"Is there something else?"

"Well, it doesn't necessarily fit your kidnapping scenario but there was a report of a young woman's body that was fished out of the water down south near the Malaysian border. The girl hasn't been identified as of now but there were some weird circumstances surrounding the death."

"Weird how?"

"She was wearing a white robe, much as a Buddhist nun might wear and her head was shaved, but she had no clothes on underneath her robes. She had drowned but her body had bruises as if she had been beaten. The forensics were somewhat confused by the fact that lizards had gotten to the body and done some feeding on it before some fishermen found it and called the police."

"Wow, this is going to get great coverage in social media."

"Well that's another unusual thing. These fishermen are not really an I-phone crowd. There were no pictures taken by them. The police arrived and blocked anyone from outside the area from coming in. Then the body was taken out secretly on an army helicopter. There are no photos or press coverage other than the brief police statement that was given out in Narathiwat forty miles away. There is nothing on social media. Apparently the police or the army are treating this as an event that didn't happen."

Matt thought for a second and then another strange angle of the girl's death occurred to him.

"Also that's Muslim country in the south. It's not an area with many Buddhist temples or religious centers. Actually that might help to identify the girl. There can't be that many places where nuns are residing down there. In any case let's put it on the back burner for now. Let's keep looking for whoever it was that took Jack's daughter."

For the first time Jade interjected.

"Well, I'm new at this, but it seems we don't have much to go on. What do we track? We've got three unidentified men who snatched a girl and disappeared in a black sedan with plates not from Bangkok."

"Yeah, you're right. Basically we have a whole lot of nothing. That leads me to think I'm going to have to get Jack to agree that I go to my police contacts on an informal basis."

Just then Matt's phone rang. It was Jack with an urgent tone in his voice.

"Khun Matt, I'm glad I got you. Listen, I'm sorry Khun Matt but I want you to stop looking for my daughter. You must stop looking for her."

"Jack, what is this? Every day is important in terms of getting her back safely. Why do you want us to stop?"

"Khun Matt you must accept what I want on this. I've received a phone call. They say my daughter is fine but they know I've asked people to look for her. They say if I don't stop the people looking they will kill her. I can't take that chance Khun Matt. You must stop. I will have to deal with them by phone. I can't talk about it anymore."

"What about John? You asked him to go after her. He's still missing you know."

"I'm sorry, but John is a professional man. He knew this search might be dangerous. I can't be responsible for him, especially if it will endanger my daughter."

"Okay Jack, I'll do as you say, but what I won't do is stop looking for John. He's my best friend. If he is in trouble I intend to be there to help him."

With that Matt hung up. Noi and Jade were staring at him. What was going on?

Matt took a second to gather his thoughts, let out a deep breath and then told them.

"Whoever is behind the kidnapping called Jack. They told him to stop looking for his daughter. They promised him she was safe but if he kept people looking for her they would kill her. He wants us to stand down."

It was obvious Jade didn't like that line. She wasn't in this for Jack's daughter, who she didn't know, or for Jack. She was concerned about John. When she spoke to Matt it was more of a challenge then a question.

"What do you intend to do?"

Matt smiled at her, as Noi watched, and gave the only answer he could.

"You know what we're going to do. We're going to find John and make sure he's okay."

Now he got the full smile from Jade but this time her eyes weren't laughing.

"Let's do it."

Noi prompted Matt. "Talk with Neung. He knows John and he will be open to helping you quietly."

Matt nodded and, looking to Jade, explained.

"Neung is my number one police contact. We went through

army ranger training together. Now he's with the Thai Department of Special Investigation, the DSI. It's their equivalent of our FBI. We've worked on some cases together. If he can help us he will and he will surely have some insights into how to investigate this further. Let me get in touch with him and set up a meeting."

"Fine. We're working together, right?"

"Right."

CHAPTER FOURTEEN

It had taken several hours of extremely slow movement in the dark, working around trees and over rocks, but John had finally moved completely around the sleeping men and their ebbing campfire and down to the dirt road. There was no way he could reach his motorbike as it was inside their encampment circle. Also he couldn't take a chance on stealing one of their motorbikes. It would make noise when he tried to start it.

At the same time, he couldn't count on walking out of the area on the dirt road. He had much too far to go and there would surely be people coming out to tap the rubber trees before too many hours passed. The rubber tappers normally started about 1 a.m., hours before the sun rose, when the rubber sap ran best. The rubber tappers probably would not be part of the gang that was looking for him but they would certainly not be open to assisting him in any way. He was an infidel as far as the locals were concerned. Why should they risk the displeasure of the men with guns to protect him?

John decided to put distance between himself and the men in the camp on foot. He went to the edge of the dirt road but not down into the shallow ditch alongside it. There was no telling what creatures where sheltering in the ditch at night and he had no desire to find out.

He walked slowly but steadily, the road started taking him gradually up hill and he remembered from the ride in that he had passed over a number of hills. He now would have to go over them again. It was a long distance to the coastal highway and the sea. There were clusters of bamboo huts with thatched roofs built on wooden pilings along the way, homes for the rubber tappers. He couldn't take a chance on walking through one of these clusters of houses. There wouldn't be dogs to wake the sleeping people, as the Muslims felt dogs were impure and wouldn't keep them, but there would be roosters, geese or ducks or whatever.

He felt himself forced to the decision. He had to get close enough to a group of houses to observe but not so close that they would notice him. He found a suitable site on the side of a group of houses well away from the camp of men who had found his motorbike and moved twenty meters up the hillside and waited.

As he expected, around 1 a.m. there was activity, dim lights, and some voices from the houses. Then some people walked out, using flashlights, mounted their motorbikes and went down the road to differing access points to the rubber plantation. It was time to start the day's process of rubber tapping. One of those motorbikes would be his ride home.

John eased down to the road and walked after the motorbikes watching their lights as they went, one by one, to differing points and parked. The tappers went into the rubber plantation on foot knowing where they had left off tapping trees the day before and where they wanted to start the new day. A couple kept going out of his sight but two bikes were within a few hundred meters walk and separated by over a hundred meters. He could pick either one. Once he was riding down the road in the darkness anyone who saw the bike would just presume it was another rubber tapper going out to work. By the time the sun rose he would be nearly back to the highway and safely away.

The rising sun sent long shadows across the dirt road and blinked its golden eye through the gaps in the rubber trees. John sped down the trail on the 125cc Honda Dream he had liberated from the rubber tapper.

He was tired but relaxed, every minute took him closer to more populated and regulated areas near the coast where he would be safe from possible confrontation with Muslim insurgents. The coastal highway was his immediate goal. He felt good. He had gotten in unobserved and except for having to leave a motorbike behind, was getting out without incident.

The trail turned as he came over a hill and he was facing almost directly into the early morning sun now. The shadows of the trees had disappeared from the road back into the rubber plantation. Then, near the next hilltop, he saw shadows that appeared to be on the road.

He pulled the bike to a stop on the side of the road, squinting into the sun, trying to make out what was going on at the next hilltop. He pulled out his binoculars. Against the glare of the sun he could make out two men. They had parked their motorbikes and were lounging against them. One was looking to the east the other towards John. The man facing John noticed him and called out something to his partner, then paused, without binoculars, they couldn't be sure who he was or what he might represent.

As John looked at their motorbikes, he saw leaning against each one an automatic rifle. At this distance he couldn't be sure exactly what model but he was sure he didn't want a closer look. It was time to head off the road, through the lanes of rubber trees to find a different way to go east and access the coastal highway. As he kick-started his bike he looked back at the two men and saw they were jumping towards their motorbikes and weapons and were going to come his way for a closer look. What the hell was this? As far as they knew he could be just a local farmer. They had no reason to chase him. In any case he decided he had to move and move fast.

John was scrambling and swearing at himself mentally at the same time. He had relaxed way too soon. Coming into the rubber plantation and jungle area leading to the hills surrounding the temple had been easy. Why did he think going out would be just as easy?

The real question was, why were they chasing him so intently? Other than leaving his motorbike behind he had left no trail. They obviously had security concerns above and beyond the normal insurgent urge to shoot at a few people here and there.

He didn't want a shootout. If two of their guys were killed, whoever they were with would be buzzing like bees when he returned and he planned to return. He didn't want to raise any undue alarms. He wasn't finished with the monks and the temple yet.

The rubber trees ran in straight parallel files and the ground between the trees was flat so the cross country going was relatively easy at first. He deliberately headed towards a hillier area, one covered by jungle growth. It would be hard for him to get through but equally hard for his pursuers and maybe they would get discouraged and turn back. They couldn't be sure who he was, possibly just a frightened local, not really worth their time.

He came to a narrow stream, took his bike into it and then decided to take it upstream. His pursuers would be able to see he hadn't crossed it but would have to guess, did he go upstream or downstream? Of course they could follow along the banks downstream to look for his exit but the thick brush growing along the stream would slow them. They would also have the option of splitting, with one going down stream on his bike and the other upstream to double check. Either option would give him a chance. If they came upstream he might be forced to shoot them.

He took his bike and started walking it upstream, up the rise of the hill. Once he killed the engine he could hear the two motorbikes of his pursuers in the distance. He only had a few minutes. He steered around some rocks in the stream and came to an area where the trees and foliage hung over the stream. He had to brush the branches back as he went through. This place would serve. He took his bike out of the stream and wheeled it a few meters off to the side where it couldn't be seen. Then he doubled back and hid in the foliage along the stream. He would ambush whoever came after him, if possible without shooting them.

From his vantage point John heard the motorbikes come to a stop at the stream. He could hear their voices as the two men discussed the situation but couldn't make out what they were saying. Just how motivated would they be, not knowing who had run from them, to push into the jungle underbrush in their chase?

Then it got quiet. John waited. Then he heard a splashing noise. One or both of his followers was walking upstream looking for him. The splashing noise stopped, then started again, getting louder. John tensed, holding his Sig Sauer ready. One of the men appeared just in front of him in the stream, his eyes searching the brush on the banks. He wasn't carrying his automatic rifle but rather was carrying a parang, the Malay version of a machete, in his hand, his rifle was slung over his back. He swiveled towards John's brushy hiding point and saw John poised to shoot.

John yelled "Drop it," but, for whatever reason, yelling a war cry, the man raised his parang to slash and launched himself towards John. John shot him twice, center of mass. One shot would probably have been enough but a lifetime of training and reflex said 'shoot twice.' The man's body fell at John's feet.

"Oh hell. Why'd you make me do that? I really didn't want to shoot you."

Immediately there was yelling from the other man waiting downstream. John maintained silence and crept slowly through the brush wanting to get to a point where he could observe further downstream. The man yelled again. John froze. Suddenly there was a stream of automatic rifle fire going over his head. He waited and then the firing was repeated again off to the side and on the other side of the stream. He had one advantage. The shooter obviously didn't have an idea where he was and was panicking and shooting all around.

John waited. The man yelled again. Then John heard a motorbike start up and ride off. Most probably the second man was going to get help.

John moved quickly but still carefully down to a vantage point where he could see his entry point to the stream. The second man was gone and there was a motorbike on the ground.

He hurried back and turned over the body of the man he'd shot. They were two holes in his chest. He was gone. "Sorry partner. You forced me to do it."

He was a young man with a bandana wrapped around his forehead but as John looked him over what he saw wasn't what he had expected. The man had no facial hair or beard as most Muslims did. Further, he had no hair on his head at all. He had been shaved including his eyebrows much as a Buddhist novice to be ordained as a monk. Whatever and whoever he was, he wasn't part of the local insurgent group that had found his motorbike. John sat back shaking his head, puzzled, again talking to the man he'd shot.

"Who are you? Who are you with? What were you protecting in this neck of the woods?"

These were questions he had better find the answers to before he even thought about coming back into these woods.

John had thought his killing days were over long ago and regretted having to shoot the man in front of him. One new aspect of the separatist activity in the south was word that some ISIS followers had joined their ranks. However, looking at the man he had shot and his dress gave John no suggestion that he was part of the local insurgent group or ISIS.

The shadows in the forest indicated it was approaching midday, but he was now committed to finding the long way out. He had to move. He got on his motorbike and rode it further into the rubber plantation taking his time now. He wanted no more surprises. He knew he would eventually come across another trail leading out of the plantation, away from the road he had been on, which would lead to another access road. He could ride that road to the coastal highway.

He was not happy. He had surely stirred up a hornet's nest but the shooting was a long way from the temple complex. They had not gotten a clear look at him. It was very possible that whoever chased him would have taken him for a local military scout looking for the insurgent camps. On the positive side he actually had more information. Not only was the temple located deep in the jungle reserve but he knew now that it was not only the local partisans who had an extensive security network around it. There was another group involved for whatever purposes. That information was only good if he could get out and share it with the right people.

Chapter Fifteen

The meeting place Neung selected was a safe house his unit kept in an area of Bangkok near the popular green spot and jogging area, the railway park in Chatuchak, that was close to his government office on Chang Wattana road. The park was a site closer to Bangkok's second airport, Don Muang, than Matt's office or usual haunts along the busy commercial Sukhumvit road corridor.

Neung, still keeping in the top physical condition that had seen him through U.S. army ranger school with Matt, liked to go for long runs at the end of the day at Chatuchak park. He would use the safe house as a place to park his car and wash up afterwards. It was convenient and secure for this meeting and he had begun find his office less and less suitable for such meetings.

Matt had at first considered meeting Neung alone but Jade had quickly objected when he raised the issue, and refused to be left out of the meeting. He had though, convinced her to leave her motorcycle behind. She rode with him and handled the navigation as Matt followed his car navigation system to the house coordinates Neung had given him.

The gate to the driveway of the house had been left open and as Matt drove in and parked, Neung opened the house door and waved them in. He then pressed a button that closed the gate behind them.

Matt had warned Neung that he was bringing a friend but he

had not given any background on Jade or their joint effort. As they entered the house Neung waved them to a dining area that had been set with tea and coffee. He then spent a minute inspecting Jade. She was again dressed all in black including the light leather jacket. It was her uniform it seemed. She withstood Neung's not too subtle inspection without blinking.

He gave Matt a faint grin, "So this is John's friend?"

Man talk. In Neung's subdued way of speaking, this was his way of saying 'Really, a girl?' much as Noi had reacted.

Matt raised his eyebrows a touch to show sympathy with Neung's perspective. He then made a fuller introduction emphasizing Jade's military background and capabilities. He summed up with the most important point, "I spoke with the people in the law office. They all said John trusted her and worked with her on sensitive and possibly dangerous jobs."

At that Neung nodded his welcome to Jade then turned back to Matt.

"Okay. What has John got involved in and how might that involve DSI?"

Matt went over the full story including Noi's research and her report that she couldn't find anything on kidnappings. He included Noi's mention of the body of a girl being found in the south and how the army had handled it with nothing being available publicly afterwards. Neung stopped him at that point.

"The girl who was kidnapped. When was this?"

"Over a week ago."

"Does she have any identifying marks or tattoos on her body?"

This question stopped Matt. He looked at Jade and could tell she had the same fear he had. Something had happened to Jack's daughter.

"I don't know. Noi spoke with her girlfriend but nothing was said of that."

"Can you call her now and ask?"

"You mean you might have something?"

"I don't know. I have some information from a colleague of

mine, the medical examiner who the army took down south to look at the body. She was unhappy with the way the army was handling things and felt they didn't respect the body. For her that respect for the dead is very important. Can you have Noi call the girlfriend and check on this? I guess it's a long shot but let's be sure."

Matt phoned Noi, gave her the request and asked her to get back to him as soon as possible.

They waited. Neung used the time to be a cop and asked Jade a few questions about her background and her service, especially her combat service. She, as always, seemed amused by such interrogations that were more an obvious questioning of her abilities. She was used to it. She gave full but brief answers. At the end it was clear Neung was impressed and reconsidering his original shock at a 'girl' being involved. Cops anywhere would be resistant. For Thai cops, women were difficult to accept as part of the team, especially on the front line. In the back office it was okay.

Turning back to Matt, Neung said, "I have to tell you that I'm in a difficult place right now at the office, so I may be limited in the help I can give you."

"Why's that?"

Now Neung turned to include Jade in his comments. "The military mafia is in charge of the country right now." He shrugged. "It happens."

He went on. "The generals are very upset with the growing financial power and popularity of a new Buddhist sect. The head of the sect, Luang Somboon, exerts enormous power well outside of the normal religious realm. The military wants to have discussions with him. He has gone into hiding. The generals are pressuring my organization, the DSI, to find him and bring him in. Unfortunately, I'm the lead agent on this matter. This leaves me very limited on being able to track other things."

Matt's phone rang. He spoke with Noi for a few minutes, hung up and turned to Neung and Jade.

"Well there is something. Apparently these two girls did everything together and of course their parents didn't know. A year ago they got matching tattoos in an area seldom exposed. Each girl got a small devil figure tattoo. The devil is laughing and holding a spear pointing towards the pubic region. The tattoo was put on their groin well below their waistline."

Neung sighed and shook his head. "Well, Matt I'm afraid the girl you're looking for is dead. That description matches the tattoo the medical examiner found on the body of the girl down south."

"What about the body? Where is it now?"

"Well that's a problem. That is the reason my colleague was upset as there won't be the proper religious rituals. As of now the army is holding it. Her death is an event that never happened."

"Why? How could her kidnapping and murder be a threat to the army?"

"Yes, why? I don't have the answer but what happened to this girl does provide me some data points in what I'm charged with now."

When Neung paused in his explanation it was Jade that interjected, "What could a religious sect possibly have to do with the kidnapping of a rich college girl?"

Neung was not used to being questioned by a woman. He gave Matt a bit of a sour look but then rolled with the punch.

"Connection? I'm not sure. This sect preaches that it's good to be rich and preaching salvation to the rich has made the sect rich and powerful. Before you came with this story, I was focusing on the possibility that there was a group within the sect, down south, smuggling to raise money. Maybe there's a connection.

Matt, wanting to keep the focus on his immediate objective, finding John, pushed the talk back to that.

"Is that where John might have gone in his search for the girl?"

"It's possible. John didn't come to me. He has many of his own sources but the leads you mentioned seem to point south.

Did he have any backup that you know of?"

"No, not that we know of and he's been out of touch for over five days now. I think it's time to be worried."

Looking to Jade, he said, "Maybe it's time we went down south."

Neung shook his head no as if in disagreement, but then said, "I've got a couple of men in Narathiwat. They can lay out the local situation for you. I'll give you their contact but be very careful. The army command there won't want civilians poking around."

"Okay. We've got some planning to do. We'll give you a call before we leave."

As Matt and Jade rose and walked towards the door, Neung called after them.

"For now don't say a word to the gambler about his daughter. Let me find where the army is keeping the body and what their plans are, okay?"

"Okay. We'll be in touch."

Chapter Sixteen

Driving back into the central part of Bangkok Matt spoke to Jade about his effort to help the girl Apple with her loan shark problem. If they were to follow John's trail and travel to the south they would surely be gone for days if not a week or more. He wanted to be able to find a way to take the pressure off of Apple before they left.

Jade's response was immediate, "Count me in."

"What do you mean count you in? You don't know what the action plan is and you don't even know Apple."

"You and this police sergeant are going to take down an asshole who's been bothering this girl right?"

"Right."

"That's all I need to know. As you guys work out the plan, count me in. The creep won't be looking for trouble from a woman. Maybe that's where I fit in."

Matt just nodded and thought to himself, hell, looking at this woman most men would expect trouble.

"Okay. Let's see what Sergeant Sombat says."

Apple had given one request to Matt and Sergeant Sombat. She asked that they not confront or arrest the loan shark at the pool bar she worked at. She wanted to avoid any connection that would invite reprisal to her workplace.

The bust was to take place the next day. Matt had agreed to meet Sergeant Sombat at Spankys pool bar on Soi 13. Spankys was where Matt had first contacted him, and it seemed a good place to discuss how the operation would be done.

Since Jade wanted to be involved Matt felt, as part of their partnership in looking for John, that this operation might be a good test case. He wanted to see how she handled herself in a pressure situation other than holding a gun on him.

The pool bar wasn't busy as they walked in and took a table on the side. They both ordered soft drinks with Jade getting a puzzled look from the waitress over Jade's Thai as a second language vocabulary. When the waitress delivered the drinks she asked Jade, "You're not Thai?"

Jade hesitated a second and then smiled at her. "Uhhh, my mom is Thai, but I grew up in America."

Matt could tell the waitress would like to have chatted a bit more with Jade but he gave her a thank you and she understood to move along.

"I take it the girls like to chat with you."

Jade gave him a slow smile, "Yeah, they want to help me with my Thai."

Then looking around she asked, "Is this where you come to shoot pool?"

"Yes and no. I have several places which have better tables and set ups. I mostly go to Hustlers in the Times Square building or Sportsman down the street here. You can find good players either place."

"And that's what you do to relax?"

"Mostly. Also Muay Thai workouts. You?"

"To relax?" Matt nodded.

"Shooting. Mostly handguns. Maybe it's like your pool. I need to really focus my mind on the mechanics and the targets and that takes my mind off of problems. I have a mixed martial arts workout routine when I feel the need."

Matt nodded and thought to himself, actually we're pretty much alike. There was no way he was going to say that though.

Sergeant Sombat came in and walked to their table. Before

he sat down he said hello to Matt and then looked at Jade who just smiled at him. She was getting the same once over and somewhat cool reception from Sombat that she had gotten from Neung. She understood. In Thailand she was a woman in a man's world.

Matt had to smile. He was beginning to understand where she got her in-your-face attitude. It helped offset the critical examinations she ran into, probably on a daily basis.

Matt made the introduction as he had done before emphasizing Jade's military background and mixed martial arts abilities. He raised the idea that she could be useful when it came time to confront the loan shark.

Sergeant Sombat smiled and just nodded to Jade before turning back to Matt.

"If you say so, but this could be dangerous. We've decided to arrest this man when he goes back to report his day's take. We've talked to several of his 'customers' and have more than enough evidence but the chief wants to see if we can roll up some of the others in the gang and get at the computer they use to keep track of their customers, their income and maybe, if they are dumb enough, their bank accounts. The way to do that is to follow him back to their collection house and raid it after he goes in. Our cover story for the press, when they find out, will be that it was a gambling raid which will actually be true as that house is also used for card games. That might give us time to roll up some of the other collection points before the word gets out."

"How can we help?"

"The police can't approach too close before it's time to go in. One of the gang might spot us. However, if a civilian couple went there and asked to get into the card games using an identification name, which we'll give you, that would be useful. Whatever the bosses there think, they won't think you're cops. Do you know how to play Texas hold 'em?"

Matt started to nod yes and before he could respond, Jade had already said, "I do." Both Matt and Sombat laughed.

"Then you get inside and do one important thing. Watch to see who goes in what direction to escape and what gets hidden as we come through the front door. These guys are always aware and ready to block intruders. It might take us five or even ten minutes to get inside. One warning. You two can't carry guns. The police will have the guns. Understand?"

"Okay."

The timing would be late afternoon the next day. The loan shark did his rounds in the afternoon and headed back to the collection point and gambling house about 4 p.m. each day. He would be under surveillance by a team of police who would warn the others on stakeout near the location. It was a mixed residential/commercial side street like many in Bangkok. The shop houses were all narrow front three- and four-story townhouse buildings as were the residences. The townhouse which served as the neighborhood gambling center and collection point appeared to be a residence, though one with a lot of foot traffic.

Matt and Jade would be with the stakeout crew and then walk over to the gambling house as soon as the loan shark went inside.

Sombat gave them the meeting point and time for the next day and, with their agreement to the plan, headed out on his rounds for the evening.

Matt was eager to head down south and get on John's trail but he and Jade could use the day prior to the raid to make their preparations and then take off after the raid if all went well.

Matt asked Jade, "Are you okay with all this? It could be dangerous?"

"That's what makes it fun. If we get to kick some jerk's ass that's all the better."

"Okay. I'll see you tomorrow. I need to spend some time with Noi and explain what's going on. She worries."

Matt was waiting to see if Jade would say she had to spend

some time with someone but she wouldn't give him that sort of background. She just smiled and said, "I've got some preparations to make too. See you tomorrow."

Chapter Seventeen

When Matt called Noi and told her he needed to spend the night at his apartment getting ready for his trip down south, she had a quick answer. "Then I'll just have to come to you, right?"

Of course the answer was yes. Though she hated it when he got involved in what she referred to as 'one of his missions,' she had adjusted to the extent that they would be together, on his terms, prior to setting off. When he got back he would go along with whatever she said were her terms for the reunion. The system worked and he was happy to have it in place. All his time in the military he had never had anyone to come home to. He found it made a real difference and he now sympathized with the married guys he had served with. As a single guy he had wondered how they could focus on the mission when the girl was waiting for you to call and reassure her you were safe. Some women didn't know how to play it cool. Some guys suffered for it. Matt at times felt it affected their performance. He didn't like it but nothing could be said.

With Noi, after some initial discussions in the early days of their relationship, she had adjusted to his mission-oriented lifestyle and learned how to play it cool. She didn't like the things he let himself get involved in, and it would always be an issue, but she had managed to help find ways to talk together and work it out.

They did have a brief discussion of the fact that Jade would be going down south with him. Matt had been concerned that it would be a problem for her and decided to tackle it head on and raise the subject first.

"You're cool with Jade going down with me right? She is John's friend after all."

"Well, let's see. She's lean and mean. She's got a short haircut. She rides a chopper. She wears leathers all the time in addition to carrying a gun. Right?"

"Right."

Eyebrow raised, "No. No problem. I can't see you riding on the back of her chopper, and I'm the only one on the back of your bike right?"

"Uhh, right."

"Good. So let's get to more important things."

The way to overcome concerns she might have was to stay together and stay close, especially before he went off on whatever mission he might have. Matt often thought those were their best nights. When you might lose love, you cling to it. On those rare occasions when Noi was angry with Matt over something, she would tell him, "All you're going to get tonight is the monkey."

When she said that, what she meant was she was in a bad mood and she was going to turn her back on him in bed. No embrace. All he would see that night was her piece of epic Indian tattoo art which included a monkey figure, 'Hanuman with Totsagan's mermaid daughter.' The elaborate tattoo covered her entire back. Departure nights were the opposite case. She understood he didn't need issues beyond what he was carrying and he didn't see the monkey until she turned over afterwards and curled up to sleep.

That night and the morning were no different. She knew the best way to support him was to act normal though she never felt that way when he went off. In the morning she had a cup of tea, gave him a quick kiss and she was off early to her software shop. No drama.

She had been upset to learn of the probable death of the girl who had been kidnapped, however. She did have one question before she left. "Do you want Plato to poke around some more on the web on this kidnapping thing?"

Plato was the resident hacker in her shop. He was overweight and full bearded and the joke was he didn't need a woman as he was married to his computer. He loved the challenge of hacking and belonged to the loose grouping of hackers resident in Bangkok. Plato found penetrating Thai government systems, when necessary, an easy chore. He was also devoted to Noi, appreciating the free rein she gave him in the office.

"Yeah. Let's not get caught, but the deeper he can go into the dark web the better. I'll check in with you when I get down south."

Chapter Eighteen

In Bangkok it seems almost every neighborhood or major apartment complex has a local gambling house. These are normally the scene of a variety of card games or mahjong, though mini casinos are also found. This was the type of gambling house that the police had identified as being used by the loan shark gang in that area of Bangkok as their clearing house.

Matt and Jade had been driven past the four-story townhouse by a plain clothes detective using his own car. Outside of some potted plants on the front sidewalk and curtains pulled on the ground floor windows, there was nothing about the house that indicated it was different in its use in any way from the neighboring townhouses on the tree-lined street. It was however an expanded version of the other houses on the street, what would have been termed a 'double wide' in an American trailer park. There was a scattering of commercial houses on the street having a business on the ground floor and living quarters for the family upstairs, and a 7-Eleven convenience store but, all in all, it was a quiet neighborhood.

The detective drove into a parking space in front of a townhouse on the end of the block. They would wait inside until word came that the loan shark who had been squeezing Apple came to report in.

Matt and Jade had met earlier at his apartment so she could park her motorcycle in his parking space while they used his

Toyota 4Runner for the trip south. His Toyota was parked in the police lot where they met the detective and were introduced by Sergeant Sombat. He had then given them the name to use when seeking entry to the gaming house. They were to say that Khun Mechai had sent them. Apparently this name was changed weekly and was only necessary if the doormen didn't know the people seeking entry.

They had to wait nearly two hours which, while normal for police work, was not normal for Jade. She would sit for a while and then get up and prowl through the ground floor of the house they stayed in. About the third time Jade got up to walk, the detective looked at Matt and Matt just shrugged. Matt and the detective had no problem staying still, both had experience, though different in nature, of waiting for things to happen. The detective's experience was in the city and Matt's in the field in differing combat situations but both knew what it was to go into a quiet mode. They waited.

While Jade prowled Matt watched her closely. No matter that John's experience with her had been good, she was still an unknown quantity to Matt. He wondered how her nerves would hold up when they went into the house. He would need to keep an eye on her.

Finally, the call came. The loan shark had just turned into the target house. The detective nodded to Matt and Jade and said, "Good luck. We'll be five minutes after you and we'll come in from the top floor as well as the front door. If you're at a table, stay sitting, if you're not, get against a wall."

Jade had nothing to say but nodded. Matt said, "Thanks. See you soon."

They had discussed how they would walk down the street and enter the house. Matt was the husband and Jade the dutiful Thai wife. She would walk behind Matt and say nothing. He would use the pass name and enter the house first. As they walked along the street they passed a vendor cooking hot Thai food on his cart. The pepper fumes bit Matt's eyes. He looked back and saw Jade having the same reaction. She smiled at him. Don't worry.

Matt approached the door but didn't have to knock. It was opened as he approached. He smiled and mentioned Khun Mechai. The doorman looked him over and then shrugged. He was muscle, he wasn't really getting paid to think. He gave Jade a longer look as she went by but it was more male curiosity than anything else. She smiled and slightly exaggerated her rump movement as she went by. That came under the heading, anything for the mission.

There were about thirty people in the expanded room with three tables going for card games. There was a small bar in one corner and, after greeting them and asking their drink order, a waitress went to bring two Sprites for Matt and Jade. The room was well lit with strip lights on the ceiling focusing on the tables. Matt and Jade stood against a wall next to a small side table on which they placed their drinks and waited for an opening at one of the tables. At the back of the room a man was sitting at a table operating a computer and counting out cash while updating information on the computer. There were two men with note-books in hand standing in front of the computer table. The man at the computer glanced at them when they ordered their drinks but no one else paid them any attention.

Jade asked the waitress where the ladies' room was. The waitress pointed out a door in back of the room opposite the computer table. She said the mens' room was upstairs.

They both took a sip of their drinks and then put them back down on the table and edged towards the wall thinking something should happen soon. Then it did. There were shouts and a loud crash from the front door followed by banging noises. The cops were breaking down the door. Yelling, screaming, cards flying, money being scooped up, people running towards the back and up the back stairs, all was in motion.

Matt saw the computer man scoop up the money on the table and push it in a bag and break for the stairs. He paused for a second, gave something to one of the waitresses and then vaulted up the stairs.

The banging noise increased and then it was the cops yelling as they came in the door. They called for everyone to stop moving. Several of the cops ran through the room and up the back stairs. Matt, following orders, froze against the wall but then Jade broke for the ladies' room and banged against the door launching herself into the room. Matt heard female yelling and screaming. One of the cops stopped outside the door uncertain as to what to do. After a minute the door opened and Jade came out with an arm lock on the waitress, pushing her into the room in front of her. The waitress's hair was askew as were her clothes, with her shirt pulled out and hanging over her skirt.

Jade smiled and handed the woman over to the cop saying, "She's yours."

The waitress turned and glared at Jade, swearing at Jade in a way the Thai call 'bak ma' or dog mouth as the cop walked her away.

Jade walked over to Matt who was staring at her, at first he was speechless, and then he said, "What the hell were you doing? We were ordered to stand fast."

Jade, a bit breathless after her struggle, gave him a grin and then asked, "You didn't notice?"

"Notice what?"

"The girl had something to hide. That's why she broke for the bathroom. I thought the male cops might be slow to follow so I went over and here's what I got." She held up a thumb drive. "The guy on the computer was worried about this and gave it her. That's when she ran for the ladies' room, so it must have some value."

"How did you get it?"

Now he got an even bigger smile. "You haven't been back in the states much in recent years have you?"

"Yeah, so what?"

"Well to paraphrase a popular saying, what happens in the

ladies' room stays in the ladies' room. Let's just say the girl couldn't hide it from me."

The detective, who had driven them over to the neighborhood, walked up and asked if everything was okay.

Matt said, "Yes, and my aggressive friend here came up with something they were trying to hide."

"What's that?"

Jade held up the thumb drive handing it over, "There must be info on this they didn't want you to have. I took it off of one of the waitresses trying to hide it. I hope it's useful."

"I'm sure it will be. Thanks. Thank both of you. You can go now. We will need some statements. Sergeant Sombat will get in touch with you. I'll have one of my men drive you back to pick up your car."

CHAPTER NINETEEN

John spent twenty minutes in the shower trying to steam off the dirt and jungle mites he had picked up in his several days' excursion into the remote area along the Malaysian border. His hotel room in Naratiwat was secure. The hotel was an older one located near the ocean, surrounded by palm trees, and was owned by an old Thai army special forces friend, General Preecha. He knew the general had some ties to the south and John had called him for guidance prior to making the trip. The manager had not been alarmed when he was a few days past his date due back from his trek into the jungle. He had been warned earlier by John just to wait as he might be held up. John was hungry and exhausted when he returned but after cleaning up and eating he had a call to make.

He called his office and left a message that he was fine. He secured the door to the room with a chair, turned to the bed and collapsed. He needed the long night's sleep and some time to recover.

At. 8 a.m the next morning, someone was pounding on the door.

It took some time for John to rouse himself from the accumulated weariness of his nights in the jungle. The early morning pounding on the door wasn't welcome.

He reached to the nightstand next to the bed and picked up his Sig Sauer. He waited a second then the pounding stopped, he heard voices and then a lighter knocking sounded and a woman's voice. "John, it's me, Jade. I'm with Matt. Are you okay?"

"I'm okay, just not awake yet. Wait a minute."

He threw on his trousers, moved the chair and opened the door.

"Hey. Good to see you guys. Come on in. How did you two find each other?"

Matt coughed, and Jade glanced at him understanding what he meant, no mention of her getting the drop on him that night. She smiled and told John, "We just bumped into each other at your apartment when we came to check on you at the same time. Serendipity."

Matt spoke up, "You had a lot of people worried John. You left word that you would be back in a couple of days. It's almost a week now. We drove a day and a night to get here. Neung's guys helped us pin down your location once we figured out you had come down south. What happened?"

"It's a little embarrassing and I'm not going discuss it without a cup of coffee. You two go down to the restaurant veranda on the ocean side and order some coffee and food. I'll be right down."

Once comfortably seated overlooking the sea, breakfast on the way, and coffee in hand, John was ready to talk.

"Tell me first how you came to be down here and then I'll tell you what I've come up with so far."

Jade nodded to Matt letting him know she wanted him to take the lead, so Matt updated John with how he came to be involved and then connected with Jade. The only thing he left out was their activity with the police on the loan shark front and the gambling den raid.

What surprised John the most was the fact that Jack had called and wanted them to stop looking for his daughter.

"Someone must have brought heavy pressure to bear on Jack. Normally the police don't scare him too much. It's just a question of how much money needs to be paid and at what level.

That means there must have been some group more powerful than the police."

Matt nodded and said, "That's why when we went looking for a second opinion we went to Neung. What we found is that he is having his own problems with the army. He's under a lot of pressure to find the monk who is in charge of the so called 'good to get rich' cult. The army wants that guy and they want to break up his organization. He has a big following and no use for the army."

"Well I went to the army but, as I told you, I contacted some-one I knew I could trust, General Preecha. He was never one of the political generals and in fact he hates them. He doesn't regard them as real soldiers. He gave me some background and guided me down here but he is very concerned. He says there is a 'special action' group in the army that the junta's top general has sanctioned. They have some sort of underground political operation taking place here in the south."

John continued, "This is a bit of a weird case. Jack didn't want the police involved. As far as he was concerned they might have been responsible and I couldn't disagree with him on that. Also there's the weird description of the kidnappers, it seems to indicate something different from our normal kidnappings."

As they had been sitting and talking, Matt and John had positioned themselves facing each other. Each had a view of the road running along the beach and the coffee shop's outdoor seating area at the back of the hotel. Jade sat between them, her back to the hotel, looking towards the sea and the strip of sand and palm trees that constituted the beach. There was a soft breeze off the ocean and just oversized ripples in the water for waves. It couldn't be quieter. At this early hour there was no one on the beach. The road, just thirty meters from the coffee shop veranda, had little traffic. This small southern town had seen a lot of bombings and violence over the years. There were few tourists and it was only the hardiest of business travelers who ventured this way.

As John talked, Matt noticed a black pickup truck, a Toyota, the dominant brand in right-hand drive Thailand, cruise to a stop at the end of the street the hotel was on. It was fifty meters away facing towards the beach road, seemingly hesitating between turning left towards them or right away from them. However, it didn't move. It was just stopped. Matt couldn't see inside the cab as the windows were dark. His alarm bells started ringing, he wondered what was going on and then the truck turned left driving along the road towards them. He could see nothing in the back of the truck but still something was stirring, it didn't feel right.

The waitress came to the table through the glass doors of the restaurant and stopped between John and Jade, diverting their attention, as she placed their food orders in front of them.

The truck picked up normal speed and Matt started to relax. When it was almost even with them the truck braked hard to a stop, the passenger window descended and a gun barrel pointed out towards them.

"Down! Down! Down!"

Matt threw the table over and hurled himself to the ground. John, moving a bit slower, followed his lead as the first burst of fire tracked along the ground towards them. The shots were wild. By stopping so quickly the truck driver had thrown the shooter off balance just enough so what should have been the killing rounds skipped up over their heads as they lay on the ground. John and Matt both had their guns out and were returning fire. Jade had grabbed the waitress, thrown her to the ground, and was lying over her to protect her body. She had her own gun in her hand but her view was blocked by the overturned table. The doors and windows of the coffee shop behind them exploded in a whirling kaleidoscope of glass shards. The waitresses and customers in the coffee shop were screaming, overturning chairs and falling to the floor.

The gunman in the truck wasn't giving up. He put in a second magazine and was tracking more carefully now. The veranda of the coffee shop had been marked out with plants along the top of a short cinderblock wall three rows high. These blocks were catching the bullets meant for John, Matt and Jade. Stone fragments from the wall were breaking off and ricocheting wildly.

Neither Matt nor John put their heads above the parapet but they raised their gun hands, unloading rounds in the direction of the truck.

Then the shooting stopped. At first they didn't move and then they heard the truck, tires squealing, as the driver floored the gas. John was near a gap in the cinderblocks and saw the truck pulling away. He fired three shots at the back of the truck just for his satisfaction.

Silence. Then renewed screaming from inside the coffee shop. Someone had been hit.

John looked around at Matt who was crouched alongside the overturned table and Jade, who was still sheltering the waitress.

"Everybody okay?"

Jade helped the waitress get up and sat her in a chair at the table. The girl was in shock, shaking and crying. Both knees were bleeding from scrapes incurred when she was forced to the ground.

Jade tended to the waitress bending down, holding her hand and looking her over for possible wounds and telling her she would be all right.

Matt, behind Jade, said, "You've got something in your back side. Don't you feel it? Turn around." She turned away from Matt so he could see better.

Matt looked her over. She had a small shard of glass sticking out of the rear of her jeans. "Hold still." He reached over and plucked it out. "We'll have to get you a tetanus shot."

She looked at the small piece of glass with a bit of her blood on it and gave Matt an intense look.

"Don't. Say. A. Thing."

Then, she holstered her pistol while still holding the waitress' hand. She rubbed the girl's shoulder to calm her, telling her

"It'll be okay." She looked at John. "Was that for you or for all of us?"

"I don't know but we better figure it out pretty quickly. You two get out of here before the cops come." Then he looked at the shells lying about, "Pick up your brass and go. I'll talk to the cops and drop the general's name. They'll be happy to conclude it was another terrorist event and it was accidental that I was here. Your presence will complicate things. Go now. Call Neung's agents here and have them find you a quiet place to hole up. I'll catch up with you."

ACT II
CHAPTER TWENTY

Neung approached the area of the restaurant on foot. He had been holding back some things from Matt and his new partner Jade. He didn't intend to deceive them but there were some details about the kidnapping of the young girl he wasn't sure about and wanted to think on.

Interpol had a liaison office in Bangkok and Neung was on his way to meet a contact, French Inspector Len LeBlanc. The Frenchman had called for the meeting.

The meeting place, Indigo, was a very good French restaurant and one of Len LeBlanc's favorites. It was located in a side nook of a small alley off of Soi Convent and was a discreet setting for a meeting.

He arrived early and did a quick surveillance of the area. Neung was amused to see that Len had arrived early also and was doing his own surveillance.

Neung called out to him across the street. "Hey Len, you're early."

Len laughed while turning to lead the way into the restaurant.

"I think it's safe. Let's get something to eat."

Nothing was allowed to interfere with the food and the wine. Only when dinner was complete did Len come to grips with the business he wanted to discuss.

"My dear colleague, I have a question. Are you familiar with the dark web?"

"Not really. The Thai police and military are focused on the internet but their primary concern is the surface web where all the social media and public networking takes place concerning political matters." Referring to a Thailand based bit coin scam that had been broken up several years earlier, Neung asked. "Why? Do you have another case of an illegitimate site being run here in Thailand?"

"We're not sure. There is a bit of activity from the dark web which came up in another case and we believe concerns your office. For security reasons, to avoid compromising an ongoing investigation, my office is sitting on the discovery. I decided on my own to share some of it with you unofficially. Handle with care please."

"Well I'm listening. What is it?"

"This site deals in sex slaves."

"Prostitution is pretty common. Can't it just be done on the open web?"

"No, this is slavery not prostitution. A sexual target, often a beautiful female model, is kidnapped, photographed in various nude poses and then put up for bids. The bidders are promised delivery to whatever holding facility they have and the object becomes their sex slave for as long as they want. Obviously those bidding are quite wealthy and have their own security arrangements. The prices are usually in the range of several hundred thousand dollars up to possibly half a million. Payment is made though the dark web."

"Who are the customers? I mean half a million dollars is a lot of money to satisfy a sex urge."

Len shook his head, "Well I imagine the desire to have a sex slave goes well beyond a mere sex urge. The money is nothing to these people. Remember, in terms of billionaires, Asia is growing them at the rate of a new one every three days. There's no limit to their ability to buy whatever they decide they want.

Supply is the issue."

"This has something to do with Thailand and the DSI?"

"Maybe I'm wrong. There hasn't been any copy in the press here, but I have reason to believe through other sources that in Bangkok there have been a number of disappearances of beautiful young women recently. Is that the case?"

Neung let out a sigh. "Oh shit. Yes. Did these girls end up on the dark web?"

"We can't be certain but the pictures I've been shown could very well be Thai models or college girls who've been out in public. You've always said you can buy anything in Thailand. This is just another step."

"So it seems. Is the web site here in Thailand?"

"We don't know yet. It doesn't need to be. The dark web can operate anywhere in the world. The product doesn't need to be co-located with the web site and often it's not. However, it's very probable the girls are being held here until the marketing process is complete and payment is made. After that, who knows? Sorry. I'll send you what access information we have but, as I say, it's limited."

"Hey, don't be sorry. You've given me all you could. Now I'll have to go to work and try to tie some pieces together. Thanks."

Driving back home Neung's thought was, *I need some help*. He was positive he couldn't go to any of his many official contacts. The army was watching everywhere and he couldn't be sure who in the government he could trust. Some high figures in the military could be involved. A general had been charged with trafficking a year before. Somehow the case had melted away as cases against high officials seemed to do.

His Interpol friend had said there were activities taking place in the dark web that involved Thailand. As Neung saw it, that meant he would have to find whatever it was by himself, using his sources, and then establish who was behind it. He had gotten all the help he could expect from Len LeBlanc.

He decided to let it ride for the night, hoping his subconscious would come up with some feasible avenue for checking further. He needed to find a way that wouldn't point back to him or the DSI.

The next morning the issue was brought closer to home when his agents in Naratiwat called to update him on the assassination attempt earlier in the morning on Matt, Jade and John. Everyone had survived, but Matt and Jade had gone into hiding until they could find out who was trying to kill them and why. It was clear that the case they were following was more than a random kidnapping.

CHAPTER TWENTY-ONE

There were two very scared, very beautiful young women sharing the room. It was not what you would expect for a room being shared by two young women of a somewhat indulged background. The room had obviously been outfitted by a man who had little understanding or concern for feminine tastes in décor. That was the least of their problems. However comfortable the room might be, it had been made clear to them that this was their holding cell.

There was a large bathroom and shower with specialty soaps and shampoos included along with a dressing table and mirror with a full line of beauty products and aids. Their captor had made it clear to them that they were expected to maintain the best possible look for the filming sessions.

As for their prison garb, they were only allowed to wear white robes and no other clothing, especially bras or panties, as they had been told they couldn't have marks on their skin from tight clothing during the photo shoots. These sessions were important. They seemed to be the main reason they were being held here. They were filmed and photographed nude in various poses. It was a form of modeling they both had experienced before but those other photo shoots had occurred in much more favorable circumstances.

A tall young man, with a shaven head, wearing a black military style uniform with no decoration, came through the door.

"Have you had your breakfast? Was everything okay?"

The girls looked at each other, though they had only been here for a few days, less than a week, they knew it was all a charade. There was only one possible answer to any question, that was yes. The other girl, the one who had tried to fight the men and received beatings for her resistance, had shown them that. Then she had disappeared. They knew compliance was their only path.

He didn't wait for their answer.

"We are going to do some more filming today."

The girls nodded their understanding.

"Today however we are going to introduce a more sexual element. You can do that can't you?"

There were no nods to this question. What did he have in mind?

Two more men came into the room. One carrying a camera and another carrying two light stands, which he began to set up focusing on the bed.

"We believe some of our customers would like to see you two beautiful ladies interacting. We will title it 'Ladies in Love.' You can do a convincing job for us can't you?"

When he had come into the room they had reflexively drawn together on the bed. Now he mocked them.

"Yes, close. Very close. That's the idea." He signaled the cameraman. "Now, let's begin. Take off each other's robe and start with some soft kisses."

He waited. When they didn't react he moved his hand towards his belt.

"Unless you need me to show you how?"

The girls immediately shook their heads. It was better that it was just the two of them on the bed.

CHAPTER TWENTY-TWO

Matt and Jade didn't have to go far to find help when John told them to leave. They moved around the back of the hotel in the opposite direction from where the truck had appeared, and rounded the corner to the next street, where Matt was confronted by a man holding a handgun down to his side. The man held up his empty hand and Matt recognized him as one of Neung's men. The man who had helped them locate John.

"Khun Matt, it's me." The man holstered his handgun and waved to Matt and Jade to follow him. He ran to a parking lot across the street where his partner was waiting at the wheel of a black sedan. "Get in back. We've going to a safe house where you can stay."

Once sitting in the back of the car Matt explained that John had stayed behind to deal with the police. Neung's man asked Matt for the keys to his 4Runner.

"One of my men will bring it along soon. Right now we need to get you out of here before you get caught up in the police bureaucracy. We'll bring Khun John over later. His friend from the army will make sure the police don't take too much of his time."

At the safe house Matt and Jade slumped in chairs staring at each other. A lot had happened in a short space of time. A lot they didn't understand.

Jade was the first to speak asking about the two DSI agents.

"Those guys were good. Did you know they were there?"

"I know Neung doesn't do things halfway. His guys have saved my ass in the past, so this isn't new."

"A good friend to have. You and John seem to have some good friends in this country."

"I've got some ranger school connections who've never let me down and John has Thai military connections, especially old special forces guys who have been just as strong for him. I'm beginning to think we'll need all of them for this job. The bad guys seem to have some serious weight behind them. By the way, how is your, uh?"

"You mean my wound?"

"Ah, yeah, your wound."

"Are you volunteering to kiss it and make it well?"

"Not really, the way I was taught that's the wrong side for kissing."

"Me too. That's something we can agree on. No need to volunteer. Let me get into the bathroom here and check it out."

Matt waited, consciously slowing his heart rate and trying to think through the numerous scenarios of who sent the shooters.

Jade came back into the room. She walked slowly, but without a limp.

"It's okay. I'll need to put some antiseptic on it when we get a chance but it won't keep me from riding my bike. Now what?"

"Wait for John. We need to put our puzzle pieces together with his. Until then kick back here and relax."

"I can do that."

CHAPTER TWENTY-THREE

The hotel coffee shop was a chaotic mess. There were upturned chairs, tables and glass all over the floor from the broken windows. There were several customers seriously wounded, more from glass cuts than bullets, who had been taken off in an ambulance. Several with minor wounds, some sobbing with shock, were still on the scene being treated and then questioned by the police.

John was having an education in Thai police procedures. He knew he couldn't leave the scene of the shooting. He was checked into the hotel. His staying would deter the police, at least for a while, of feeling the need to chase down the man and the woman who were seen at the table with him. When asked, he had told the police they were a Thai couple whom he had greeted and was talking with. Just an accidental encounter.

Even though John had helped to tend to the wounded prior to the arrival of the police, they were not happy to have a foreigner with a gun present at the scene of the shooting. A mid-level officer soon arrived. He had two of his men hold John and take his handgun away. After that he didn't know what to do with John and had them sit him in a corner. The course of action if John had been a local resident would have been to take him down to the station for some strong talk but John presented a potentially serious public affairs problem. From a Thai cop's point of view foreigners were nothing but trouble.

94

What the police didn't fully grasp was John's command of the Thai language. He was able to track all the discussions. As the various levels of police command arrived they were quickly briefed on the situation including answering the question of "What the hell is the foreigner doing here." The first answer was that he was just a tourist from Bangkok. Though the fact that he had been carrying a gun complicated things, even though he had a permit. Then after checking the gun and finding it had been fired they upped the level of inspection. One officer went to see that he was indeed checked into the hotel. John thought, well I'm on the hot seat. The serious looks in his direction increased when the officer that had checked that he was registered at the hotel, came back and reported that the hotel was owned by an army general. This posed another major problem for the police. Who might they offend if they took John into the station?

John sat and waited as a succession of police officers of increasing rank came in, were briefed, looked at him with a pained expression and then ignored him. He had to be somebody else's problem. He was as much a leper as those who were once to be found begging on the streets of Bangkok. None of the police wanted to touch him in any way.

None of that bothered him. What was working on him was a simple question Jade had raised. Was the shooting for him, for Matt and Jade, or for all of them? If, as John thought, he was the target, who had pointed the shooter in his direction? Matt and Jade had just arrived in town and were being guided by two DSI agents. It was possible that they had been followed from Bangkok but it seemed improbable that someone could set up the shooting so quickly. No, it made more sense that the shooting was directed at him, but then, who was behind it? Who knew he was here? Who knew what he was looking into? He didn't like the direction those questions were taking him.

Finally, an army colonel, wearing special forces insignia on his uniform, came in, glanced at John sitting in the corner, and went over to talk to the senior police officer on the scene. John felt a sense of relief. The officer was Colonel Anong, a man John knew from some of his past work with the special forces. There was a bit of head shaking on the part of the police officer but finally he nodded assent.

The colonel walked over to John and said hello.

"Are you okay? The police tell me you were in the middle of the shooting. The thing is they are not sure whether you were the target or if it was a terrorist attack against the hotel."

John smiled at the colonel and shook his head. "It's good to see you Colonel. I'm fine. It seems the terrorists are everywhere nowadays, aren't they?"

Colonel Anong held John's eyes for a moment and gave the slightest of nods. He didn't believe it was terrorists, but that wasn't for him to explore.

"My orders from General Preecha are to assist you to check out of this hotel. Then I'll take you to a safer location. I told the police you'll be available later if they have more questions. Your gun will have to stay with them for now. You understand, it's a face thing. They're embarrassed enough to have had the shooting take place here."

John paused. He really wanted to connect back up with Matt and Jade but they weren't known to his friend the general and his local contacts and, for some reason, he thought it best to keep them separate from his special forces contacts for now.

"That's fine Colonel. I appreciate your help. Let's go."

Chapter Twenty-Four

Neung needed some help understanding the violence that John, Matt and Jade had run into down south. He knew how the investigation would track. The police in the south would defer to the army lead and the investigation would be limited. The army would quickly blame the separatist movement. It was convenient to label it 'domestic terrorism.' To Neung the real mystery was, who in the army was calling the shots.

His go-to guy for inside information on the army was his buddy Tommy, now an army colonel. He was Matt and Neung's buddy from their ranger course years ago. Tommy's dad was a retired general. He was not one of the power clique but he would have given Tommy all the inside information on who was happy with the junta and who was not.

Normally, when they met, Neung and Tommy would go to one of the army clubs in Bangkok. The clubs provided a private setting both were comfortable in, but not today. Neung also didn't want to use one of the DSI safe houses.

The most private venue happened to be the condo where Tommy kept rooms for his *mia noi* or 'minor wife.' The young lady was used to this interruption of her routine and accepted it willingly, given adequate warning and some pocket money for shopping with her girlfriends. She was always happy to vacate for a while.

Neung needed the real inside information on what was

happening with the internal politics of the army. The big picture was public knowledge, a group of generals had taken over the government, what was new? The current gang had held on to power for four years now.

Obviously the civilian elite had lost big time but who in the military were unhappy with the division of spoils? Who might be secretly, or not so secretly, seeking to undermine the generals who had emerged on top? Was this connected to the unrest in the South?

When they met, Neung explained to Tommy the state of play in Naratiwat. He described John's search for the kidnapped daughter of a gambling kingpin, the tip John had followed about a hidden religious base in the jungle near the Malaysian border and then the subsequent shootings including the most recent assassination attempt at the beachside hotel with Matt and his new friend Jade present.

Neung was worked up. He stood and walked around the room.

"Where I'm stuck is the simple question. Who is behind these shooters? My thinking is they can't be the Muslim insurrections the army always wants to blame. All this has nothing to do with their usual tactics and targets. I'm sure it's not the police, the police are too dominated by the army to be behind this. So that leaves me with the army. There may be a connection with the Buddhist religious cult but I don't have anything solid."

He paused, and sat back down facing Tommy.

"What can connect a faction from the army with kidnapped and, in at least one case, murdered girls, and possible secret religious bases in the south?"

Tommy shook his head, "I can't help you with the kidnapping angle. That army general you guys caught trafficking a couple of years ago was a known loser. He was stupid enough to think that any Bangkok police in his gang that were arrested would be too afraid of him to talk. They weren't. If there is a new kidnapping activity and an army faction is involved, the real motivation isn't the kidnapping, I'd look at the involvement of this religious cult."

"So we have a religious cult kidnapping young girls? No ransom payments have been called for as far as we know. Is it a sex slavery operation? Also how do we explain the number of guys carrying guns and the shootings? There has to be an army angle because I sure don't see the young monks in the cult being that handy with the gun play."

"Well, you'll have to work out the details, but there is an army general who is seriously unhappy with the junta. That's Major General Preecha, the former special forces commander. He is supposedly retired, forced out by the junta, but the special forces are still loyal and the units respond to him. He hates the junta leadership. The junta has virtually declared war on this Buddhist cult and it's possible that Major General Preecha sees this cult as an ally. The enemy of my enemy is my friend as they say. I don't see his troops kidnapping anyone but he would be happy to assist the cult to undermine the junta or maybe use the cult to embarrass them and chip away at their power."

"If that's the case, John may have a problem. That's who John was talking to about tracking the kidnapped girls down to the south. I'll have to get in touch with him and warn him to watch his back."

CHAPTER TWENTY-FIVE

Jade prowled, much as she did while waiting for the police to give the word to go ahead on the loan shark raid in Bangkok. Matt decided that 'prowl' was the fitting word for what she had been doing for the few hours they had been inside the safe house. Apparently this was her idea of relaxing.

She moved through all the rooms in the house, upstairs checking the bedrooms, looking out the back and to the sides to check the layout of the neighborhood, back through the kitchen and then the front rooms. She'd pause, sit for a few minutes, and then repeat the pattern. She was pumped up. She was always pumped up before, during and after any action. She found, within reason, it worked for her. Controlled agression had definitely helped her martial arts game over the years. She respected Matt's trained hunter instincts, but it was not her style.

Matt let it go on for a while watching from his perch on an easy chair in the front room. Finally, on one of her return visits he felt compelled to speak.

"I always felt sorry for the animals in the zoo. I felt sorry for all of them as they belonged in the wild not in cages but I felt the most for the carnivores. They are born to hunt. They are born to move over a wide hunting range but they can't because of the bars. All they can do is prowl, walk back and forth and back and forth. Frustrated animals. Tell me Ms. Jade, are you a frustrated carnivore?"

As she turned to face him, hands on hips, she had no grin on her face or smiles in her eyes this time. "You dam betcha. We're supposed to be doing the hunting. Instead we're boxed up here hiding. Aren't you just a little frustrated?"

"I am, but it's not hunting time right now. It's learning time. We need to learn who's doing the shooting and why. Until we have some idea of all that, laying low would seem to be best."

Matt's phone rang, it was Neung.

"Hey Matt, my agents reported on the shooting. Are you and your friend okay?"

"Yeah Jade and I are fine, but we haven't heard from John yet. I don't know what his situation is."

"I don't either. I understand the police released him to a special forces colonel but where they took him we don't know."

"Well, he's in the hands of friends right?"

"Aahhh, that seems to be open to question. I just finished a talk with Tommy. From what he says, who are friends and who aren't friends seems to be a bit unclear. Tommy says John's special forces contact, General Preecha, is set against the junta and may be part of the trouble you're checking on down there. What that means for John's situation is not completely clear."

"Do you have any idea who was behind the shooting or is that not completely clear also?"

Neung laughed, "Not completely clear would be a good summary. I wouldn't think the cult John was looking at is up to that kind of shooting, but they could have hired it out. It's doubtful it was the police. The army is the best suspect but what group within the army, for or against the junta, Tommy couldn't say. When you talk with John though tell him to rethink his special forces connection."

"Any suggestions on our next move?"

"Right now I wouldn't move until we find out what happened to John. He might have more information. If he doesn't show up soon I'll send more men down to help look for him but there is really nothing we can do unless the army decides to cooperate."

"Okay. We'll stay put. Your guys are in the best position to nose around, but get back to us as soon as you can. We need to make a plan and start working it. If John doesn't show up, we should begin looking for him with his special forces friends."

"I agree. Hey Matt, don't hang up yet. I have a web matter that needs looking into and I don't want to go to official sources here in Bangkok. I think your friend, Noi, might be in a position to help on this."

Neung went through his conversation with Len LeBlanc, the Interpol officer, outlining the discovery that had been made concerning a dark web site dealing in Thai women as sex slaves.

"I know her office has a couple of the best hackers in Thailand. Can you get one of them to follow up on this lead from Interpol? I need an off-the-books way to isolate the site and find a way to take it down."

"I've already asked Noi to have her best guy do some digging. I'll give him the background you gave me. He'll be happy to dive deeper. That's what he does for fun."

While Matt and Neung talked, across town John thanked the colonel for his help and dumped his gear on the bed in the room the colonel had taken him to. It wasn't a hotel but rather an eight-story condominium a few blocks from the ocean front and on the edge of town. When they entered the lobby he saw two special forces soldiers with automatic rifles standing guard.

As they passed the soldiers the colonel said, "These men will be here to insure your security. For now, it's best that you keep to your room. Just call and we'll arrange for food to be brought in."

The feeling that something wasn't right intensified, but John just nodded and thanked the colonel for his help. In the room he went to the window and looked towards the street below. There was a military vehicle parked with two more men sitting inside.

This felt more like a jail than a safe house. He decided he needed to move on his own and get back in touch with Matt and Jade. He would make do without the colonel's protection. He took the few things he needed for a couple of days camping from his bag and threw them in a backpack. Leaving his bag on the bed, he went to the door of his room and checked the hallway. Clear. He went to the emergency exit stairwell that had windows to the outside. At the back of the condo was a narrow walkway between the building and a six-foot cinder block wall enclosing the empty lot adjacent to the hotel. It looked easily scalable.

John paused at the top of stairwell, listened, and was about to descend the stairs when he heard muffled voices and smelled cigarette smoke wafting upwards.

No go. John returned to his room. He would have to ride it out. He was protected, he mused, protected from taking any action that his special forces friends didn't want.

CHAPTER TWENTY-SIX

There was a knock on the door at 9 a.m. and the two girls, May and Jum, struggled to wake up. A guard in a black uniform brought in a breakfast tray and told them they were to eat first and then get cleaned up. An important visitor was expected. They were to go through the wardrobe in their room and pick out one of the black dresses that had been provided. No underwear was to be worn.

The girls were emotionally exhausted and thoroughly humiliated. The filming session had lasted over three hours with the black uniformed director demanding more and more explicit behavior and for them to exhibit stronger external signs of pleasures they didn't feel.

At the end of the night, as the cameraman, his helper and the director left, the girls had collapsed in tears, wordless, sobbing, without hope.

Now, as they had learned to do, they began moving to follow the orders they'd been given.

As they dressed, May and Jum could hear the sound of a helicopter landing, throbbing through the structure of the building where they were being held. The sound and vibrations decreased gradually and then stopped. They sat and waited.

When the door opened they looked up expecting to see their 'special visitor' but it was only the guard in the black uniform who had supervised their previous photography sessions. He was accompanied by two men dressed similarly in black, together with a woman in white medical clothing. He told them to stand and put on the spike heels that were part of the wardrobe provided with the room.

"Follow me."

He led, and the two men and the woman followed behind the girls. They walked out of the room and down an empty corridor, past the door to the next room in which they had heard some girls crying several nights previously. But now all was deathly still. Were the girls still there? If not, what had happened to them?

The corridor came to a right-angle turn. Their guide opened a door just around the corner and showed them into a brightly lit room with beige walls. In the middle of the room were two square model pedestals, two feet off the ground with steps in front. On the wall to the side was a large glass mirror. There was no other furniture.

"Get on the pedestals and pose." He pointed to blond-haired May. "You're model one." He pointed to black-haired Jum. "You're model two. Both of you just follow directions and you'll be fine." He left the room closing the door behind him.

The girls looked at each other, both uncertain, but they had become accustomed to doing as they were told. Survival lay in compliance. They stepped up to the pedestals and struck modeling poses, one foot forward, one hand on the hip facing the mirror. It took no imagination to understand that they were being observed through a one-way glass mirror.

There was a scratching sound and then a new voice came over a speaker mounted in the ceiling. "Turn around please." It was English but definitely English as a second language.

The girls both turned and posed with their backs to the mirror.

"Step forward and turn back and take a step towards the mirror."

The girls did as directed.

"Drop the tops of your dresses to your waists. Show me your breasts."

The girls glanced at each other again, but then both complied, standing with the tops of their dresses in hand, breasts thrust towards the mirror.

"Model one, a half-turn to the right please. Ahhh, good. Hold that for a second."

Then the speaker went silent. The girls waited and then pulled their tops back up.

The door opened and a guard appeared. He pointed to May. "Come with me." He nodded to Jum. "You wait here for a while, I'll be back for you."

The woman in the medical uniform joined the guard to escort May. They took her to a room further down the leg of the corridor. This room was brightly lit and completely white. It had the appearance of a doctor's office with a desk on one side and an examining table on the other.

The woman told May to sit in the chair next to the desk. She took the girl's hand to comfort her.

"Don't worry honey. You should already be relaxed. You ate your breakfast, didn't you?"

"Yes."

"Do you ever get motion sickness?"

"No."

"Are you allergic to any medicine?"

"I don't think so."

There was a pill and a glass of water on the desk. The woman gave the girl the pill and held up the glass.

"Here take this. It won't hurt you I promise. It's just to help you relax. We're going to take you home and it may be a bumpy ride."

May complied.

Ten minutes later the helicopter took off and headed out to sea. May was going home, to her new home. The helicopter was flying to a rendezvous with a very large yacht owned by an ultra-rich person who could afford whatever he wanted. At the moment May was what he wanted.

CHAPTER TWENTY-SEVEN

This time it was Jade's phone that rang. At first, she assumed it was John calling to explain his situation but it was a new number. She was a little irritated at being bothered by a 'not John' phone call.

"Yeah?"

"Is this Khun Jade?"

"Yes, who is this?"

"Khun Jade, I'm a nurse calling from Bangkok hospital. We have a woman patient here who says she is your friend and asked us to call you."

"Can I talk with her?"

"No. That's part of the problem. Her jaw may be broken. She can't really speak clearly right now. She wrote your name and number for us."

"What happened to her?"

"We don't know for sure. Somebody beat her up, very badly. She was left in front of the hospital last night, unconscious."

"What's her name?"

"The nickname she wrote down is Apple."

"Oh shit, hold on for a minute."

Jade turned to Matt who had been watching.

"It's Apple. The girl we thought we helped with the loan sharks. Well it looks like we didn't help her enough. Somebody got to her and just beat the hell out of her. She's in Bangkok hospital with a possible broken jaw."

"Damn it. So much for the cops keeping an eye on her and protecting her." Matt paused. "One of us will have to go and look after her."

Jade held the phone back to her ear. "Thank you for calling. I'm a friend but I'm out of town. Someone will be at the hospital in a few hours and we'll take care of her bill. Please look after her."

She closed the phone and looked at Matt. "Apparently we didn't get all of the asshole loan sharks. What do we do?"

Matt studied Jade for a minute, knowing what he wanted but needing it to come from her. He raised the question.

"It seems we have some unfinished business. What do you want to do?"

"Finish it. Are you suggesting we go back and look after Apple?"

"I think one of us should."

"And that one is me? What about looking after John?"

Matt waved his arm at the immediate world outside their door. "I don't doubt how competent you are, but some of these people know me. They don't know you."

Jade studied the floor, torn between two people in different places she felt responsible for. "Okay. I'll go back to Bangkok, look after Apple and deal with the loan shark assholes."

She looked up at Matt. "You make sure to get John out of whatever mess he's in right? Let me know what's going on?"

Matt nodded. "Deal."

CHAPTER TWENTY-EIGHT

The walls and ceiling of the room were white, giving it somewhat of a hospital room appearance. The oxygen tanks at one side of the bed also contributed to that effect. There was however lush, beige carpeting on the floor, and the bed was king size and comfortable, something that would seem in place in a four- or five-star hotel. The bed covers were in disarray and there were two persons lying on the bed. The door was closed and the room was quiet except for the slow breathing of the two occupants of the bed.

Leung Somboon, looked down at the slim body of the now sleeping boy he had just finished using. He was disturbed, but not with the boy. The boy had been responsive and pleased the elder monk as he had been taught. He had been resistant in his early days at the temple, much as Leung Somboon had been when his desperately poor farming family had first given him up to the care of a rural temple. The boy now accepted that to be used by the older man was his fate. Just as Leung Somboon had eventually accepted his fate when the senior monk took him when he was first brought to the remote country temple so many years ago.

What concerned the elder monk was a feeling that too many mistakes were being made by his acolytes. He was the founder, the visionary. He was the financial whiz who had married the God of wealth creation with the religious cover of Buddhism which traditionally decreed abstention from the pleasures of this world. He felt he had not lost the way, rather he had found a new way and a message that resounded with the middle class. He had complete control within the world of his followers but now external events, beyond his control, threatened his empire.

Leung Somboon was not directly involved in the various money-making activities of his sect. It would be beneath him. At the same time, he expected all the workings of his staff to function smoothly. The comforts of the riches that flowed to the sect were important to him, increasingly so as he aged.

He left the boy sleeping. He dressed and moved to a desk and chair in an adjoining room which functioned as his workspace and called in his deputy, Arak.

"What have you been able to find out about the shooting that occurred in the rubber plantation? Have we tracked whoever it was that came in from outside?"

"Our police contacts are sure it was the foreigner who had been asking questions in town. He was gone for several days and came back to his hotel covered in dirt."

"Who is behind him? Why has he come here?"

"He may have some connection to the army. He is staying at General Preecha's hotel. It's not yet clear what the connection to General Preecha may be. We took steps to have the foreigner eliminated. Some former army soldiers for hire were sent to handle him. Unfortunately, it seems they missed. The police let the army take him away. We're trying to find out where they are hiding him."

Leung Somboon stood and glared at his deputy. "First we allow the body of the girl being disciplined to be found on the beach. That was unforgiveable. Now this shooting on the road to the temple. It's inconceivable that someone would come all the way from Bangkok searching for missing nightclub girls. Something else is going. It has to be the generals."

Arak just nodded. He had learned not to try and anticipate where the elder monk's anger would take him.

"It has to be the generals. It means they'll be coming after us here."

Leung Somboon's temple hideaway in the jungle had served well but it was not the most comfortable of places. His chain of devotees had grown to encompass many cities though out the world. He had many options. It was time to work through the possibilities and pick a site, one offering a bit more comfort and security than this one.

"Arak make arrangements for us to be picked up. I think it's time to find a more secure base. I'll contact my friends overseas myself."

CHAPTER TWENTY-NINE

John had spent a quiet night. He had no choice, as far as his special forces friends, or captors depending on how positive or negative he felt, were concerned; quiet was the only option possible. His dinner and breakfast had been brought in by a maid who had been accompanied by one of the guards who watched from the door. The routine was repeated later as the dishes were cleared away. The breakfast guard told him the colonel would be in to talk with him 'soon.'

When the colonel finally arrived a few hours later John was steaming. He started to complain about wasting time but the colonel held up a hand.

"I know Kuhn John, but I'm sure you understand. I follow orders. My orders were to keep you safe until General Preecha could talk to you. I've done so and General Preecha is available to speak with you now. I appreciate your patience. We just have to drive a short way. Come with me. My men will bring your bags."

Downstairs three military humvees were waiting. John was directed to a back seat in the middle vehicle. The Colonel climbed in the front and told the driver to go.

They drove out of the town, first on the main highway south and then, after thirty minutes, west towards the jungle-covered hills John had scouted just a couple of days before. The thought crossed his mind that they were headed towards the hidden temple/fortress area that he had already scouted out but the humvees turned up a dirt road well before the entry and exit points he had used before.

The road twisted through a rubber plantation and then entered a jungle area as it went uphill. The dirt road was a red scar through the jungle and became narrower with deep drainage ditches on both sides. At points the trees hung over the road creating a green tunnel effect brightened by sunlight blinking through gaps in the foliage. The humvees stopped at a checkpoint manned by two armed special forces troops who emerged from a roughly constructed wooden guardhouse alongside the road. The colonel talked to them and they were waved through. After another one hundred meters they came to an opening cleared in the jungle. They drove in and parked in front of a two-story villa set against the hillside and facing east towards the ocean behind them. The villa was constructed with a log exterior and a long covered front porch set with several easy chairs and tables. In one of the chairs, drinking his morning coffee, sat Major General Preecha.

The general, dressed in casual civilian clothes as if he was just leaving for a round of golf, rose as John got out of the humvee, came down the stairs and, coffee in hand, approached John.

"Khun John, welcome. I'm sorry you had to spend a quiet day and night at my condo building in town. Come, have a cup of coffee with me and I will explain what I know of how we came to be in this situation."

As John walked slowly up to sit in the porch chair the general indicated, he looked around. There was a metal shed to the side of the building and electric lines running from it to the house. He could hear the generator running. A phone tower stood watch behind the house. It all appeared somewhat new and rough but it also appeared completely connected to the outside world. John thought to himself, *Why this investment? What is the general up to down here?*

The general, a tall man for a Thai, approaching six feet in height, had put on a little weight but still had the slim build of his younger wartime years. However, his back and knees had been damaged by a few too many jarring parachute landing falls. He moved slowly.

He stood at the porch railing, looking out over the entrance road towards the ocean. "You know the fact that we can see the ocean from here makes the feng shui very good. It would be a perfect burial ground for the Chinese to have their graves facing the sun as it rises over the ocean each day. Maybe that should be my next venture. Graveyard development." He turned and smiled somewhat grimly at John, "You know I've helped put enough people in their graves over the years. It would seem a logical extension."

Then he sat down facing John shaking his head and, somewhat ruefully, asked, "What did you do?"

John knew the general well enough to know he wasn't really looking for an answer but just wanted to introduce whatever point it was that was bothering him. John didn't want to play his game.

He replied, "I think the real question, my friend, is what are you doing?"

He continued. "You told me it might well be productive for me to look into a possible jungle hideout down here that might be used to detain kidnapped girls. You somehow failed to mention that you and your supporters had a significant presence down here. I found what I believe is the hideout but what are you hiding?"

"You know John, in a funny way it's comforting. You are the only one who can still talk to me like that. None of these young soldiers would dream of confronting me. I understand I do need that at times. So thank you, but John, finding the hideaway these stupid monks have set up down here is one thing, killing one of their guards is another. They have many police on their payroll. It wasn't hard for them to track you down afterwards. I didn't know about their attempt to kill you. Believe me if my black shirt boys were involved you wouldn't be here now. Did you really have to kill the boy?"

"I'm not happy about it but unfortunately I did. It's hard to reason with murderous religious fervor. That's why the U.S. army realized that a .45 caliber pistol was necessary for the war against the Philippine insurrections over a hundred years ago. It helped to resolve religious arguments. The kid was intent on killing me. I had no choice. However, your point is well taken. I've lost a step or two over the years otherwise I wouldn't have found myself in that position. Believe me, I'm not happy about it. However, the question remains, you've got a lot more happening down here than you shared with me. What is going on?"

The general, showing his respect for John, leaned over and poured him a cup of coffee.

"Have this, it's a good mountain blend from up in the north. It will relax you."

He continued, "As for my activities here, well let's just say this is a convenient way for me to show my disgust with the generals of the junta. I have no use for these crazy monks except for the fact that they are scaring the hell out of these deskbound generals who have taken over our government. The monks approached me on a very confidential basis, said they were setting up a retreat, as they called it, down here in the jungle. They were concerned about security and asked if I could provide troops for that purpose. I told them no, I wouldn't provide them troops but my men could help to train some of their more fervent young people to provide their own security. That is what we did."

"You are telling me you had no idea of the things they've been doing to raise money for the crazy monk running the organization?"

"No, not really. I was just happy to see them embarrassing the junta. Of course I knew they have been running all sorts of money-making efforts. Scams, is that what you Americans call them?"

"Yeah, scams would be a good word but their current efforts seem to go far beyond mere scams."

The general had been sitting back, relaxed, drinking his coffee. But now he sat up and put his coffee down, facing John more directly.

"Yes, I used you my friend but it was in the direction you wanted to go. I have never been to their fortress in the jungle. I had no idea what uses they were making of it. It wasn't until you raised the possibility of this mad monk running a kidnapping scheme that I had any idea they would go that far. I could think of no one better qualified to track them down and observe their activities since you were already on the trail."

John shook his head. "I shouldn't be surprised. You always were a great clandestine operator. Okay. Where do we go from here?"

"John I got you out of the hands of the police. The monk will still want you dead but no one knows where you are so you have some advantage. If you want to go back to Bangkok, I'll have my men take you back. For my part I now stand back. I oppose the junta but I can't be too visible in my activities. I wish you luck but this is not my fight."

"Well I haven't finished my mission so I won't be leaving. Let me make a few phone calls, and I'll get out of your way. Thanks for getting me away from the police. Getting stuck in the jail here would have been embarrassing."

The general reached down to a canvas bag lying on the porch next to his chair. "Here's your handgun John, but I think you'll need much more than this if you intend to go back to the monk's fortress."

CHAPTER THIRTY

Noi's office was normally a quiet place, virtually all the computer techs would lose themselves in the screens in front of them. Sometimes, if she liked the singer or group that the staff wanted to play, she would let them play some of their choices for background music.

Today was no exception, the morning passed smoothly until there was a shout from the back of the room, away from her small office. She rose to see what the fuss was and saw Plato standing beside his computer looking towards her office. He waved to her to come over.

As Noi approached, Plato sat back down at his computer and then swiveled his chair towards her and invited her to scan the screen.

He pointed at a corner of the screen. "Do you see it?"

Noi squinted and tried to focus. There was a lot of text concerning payment options and directions. There was too much data distracting her.

"What?"

Plato pointed again this time putting his forefinger on the screen.

"Here. I don't know if the guy was stoned or what but, after putting up excellent encryption walls protecting his communications and site, he gives out his everyday hot-mail address. This can be tracked. This is just the first thread. We've got the son of a bitch running this site and probably much more. It's unbeliev-able. He's ours if you want him."

Noi pulled over a chair and sat down.

"Well he's wanted for sure. Walk me through this, keep a record. I need to talk with Matt and Neung. I'm sure they'll pass it on to someone who will do something with it."

CHAPTER THIRTY-ONE

As the new day broke, Jade was gone. Neung's men had arranged a car to drive her back to Bangkok immediately the night before. Matt was relieved. It wasn't that he could only work alone, it was just that she was still new to him and this situation suddenly looked a lot more complicated than a search for a missing girl.

Neung's men had no word on John or his whereabouts. Matt, despite his advice to Jade the day before that watchful waiting was the order of the day, was feeling the strong need to take some action.

There was one group that he trusted due the fact that he had previously fought alongside them in the jungle, that was the Border Patrol Police. On a day to day basis these special police had more encounters with armed criminals, smugglers of all types, than any other uniformed force in Thailand. They were considered the special ops unit in the national police force and took pride in being a unique force. In Matt's work with them a few years before, tracking down a yakuza gang in a jungle area in the north, he had made some good friends, especially Sgt. Major Chatri. The sergeant major was a legendary fighter with the Border Patrol Police and now assigned with the army at a headquarters post in Bangkok. This was who he decided to turn to for guidance.

The sergeant major answered on the first tones of the phone as Matt knew he would.

"Sgt. Major, this is Matt Chance. How are you?"

"I'm fine Khun Matt. How are you? Where are you?"

"Down south. Naratiwat. There are some things going on that John and I are looking into. We'll need some help. Can I give you a briefing?"

"Whatever help you and Khun John need we can do it. There's a very good Border Patrol unit down there. The men in charge are friends."

Matt went on to brief the sergeant major. He knew he would get all the help he and John needed.

CHAPTER THIRTY-TWO

In Bangkok, a narrow alleyway connected the Sukhumvit avenue side streets of Soi 11 and Soi 13—both busy nighttime venues. The alleyway was dimly lit but the lights from the shop fronts of the seediest of massage parlors running along it provided some illumination. The girls sitting on stools in front of the shops, waving to potential customers, were well along in their prostitution careers, aged in their mid-thirties to forties. They were beyond any enticing gestures other than a hapless wave of the hand and a call of 'massage' as they looked up briefly from their mobile phone fascination. Their customers would find them, or not. It was what it was.

There was a dogleg in the alleyway halfway between the two side streets. Some discord in property lines drawn long ago had left the two alley pathways a few meters off center. At this point there was also a third path, a dark offshoot from the main alleyway, which continued unlit for thirty meters to the edge of the parking area of the ancient Ambassador hotel. This walkway was seldom taken at night.

It was at this three-way junction that Jade waited. The party noises from Soi 11 and Soi 13 barely reached this deep into the alleyway. Without lighting it had the muted visibility of a confessional booth with brief flashes of the neon party lights outside showing the presence of the penitent occupant.

She hadn't been aware of the alleyway nor the dark path

branching off of it to the Ambassador hotel. She had been told of it by the female manager of the pool bar at which Apple worked when she went to get background on Apple's beating. Normally this was a safe walkway, even late at night. With the exception of pick pocket gangs, Bangkok was not a city of street crime. Confrontation was not normally the Thai criminal modus vivendi; various forms of cheating, graft or possibly burglary were much preferred.

When she had visited Apple in the hospital Jade could see the shadows of fear still in her eyes. The beating had ended but the dread it spawned would live with Apple for a long time, draining hope from her spirit. Jade had held her hand and promised that all would be okay but Apple wasn't responsive. Jade could see the accusation in her manner. She had been promised that all would be okay once before. She had believed it, but the pain had followed quickly thereafter. She felt betrayed.

The loan shark gang had been put away. They were now behind bars. The cops had done that part fine. One of the men however, the one who had originally threatened Apple, made a call from the prison to a cousin, a dimwitted hunk of muscle named App who wanted to prove himself to the gang. Here was his chance. Take care of some gang business. Deal with Apple. Make her an example.

Jade waited in the flickering shadows of the walkway. Her man would be coming along soon. He was a bouncer at a bar, Game Day, owned by an American motorcycle club, the Outlaws, from Oakland, California. The bar was located next to the Nana train stop on Sukhumvit avenue and adjacent to the Soi 11 side street. App's shift ended at 2 a.m. Then he would walk over to the pool bars on Soi 13, using the convenient alleyway as a shortcut. The manager at the pool bar said he came every night at the same time. He shot pool until 4 a.m. in their killer pool competition. The last player left at the table, missing the fewest balls, wins the cash pot. He never won but wouldn't pay for his drinks so he came out ahead. No one liked him but as he was known to be connected to the loan shark mob, no one would challenge him.

App didn't just walk, he swaggered his way along the night streets of Bangkok. To give him his due, part of it was because of the muscles he had built up in the gym in his steroid fueled quest for muscle mass. He wasn't tall, only five feet eight inches but he had managed to bulk up his frame so that he needed more space on the narrow sidewalks. All who came along gave way to him.

As he walked through the alleyway his head was down just thinking of how good that first beer would be. There was no one around, the massage shops were closing. The girls who hadn't made enough money yet had gone out to the main Sukhumvit road, in one last grab for a customer. He noted the whore standing in the dark on the side of the alley but ignored her. If she was too ugly to get out on the street and compete with the other girls she was too ugly for him. He went to brush past.

Jade didn't play the 'hey you' game. Talking was for beginners and dumb pugs. As App negotiated the dogleg and started down the alleyway to Soi 13 she was standing there as he went to brush past her. She hit him hard on the left side of the head just ahead of his ear. App didn't fall but was completely stunned and staggered a step or so to the side. Jade didn't wait but delivered the blow she really wanted to give as he stood there, a swinging kick with her left foot to the right side of his head. She had practiced this so many times and it felt good. This time App went down hard, hitting his head on the pavement. Only partially conscious, he wasn't going to be getting up soon. Jade leaned over him and put the methamphetamine pills in his shirt pocket. This was the Ya-Ice so popular with the bar girls. She started to leave, but then stopped and went back and gave him a strong kick in the ribs. He moaned but didn't move. Now she backed off towards Soi 13, while screaming "Help!" for the police and blowing a whistle. She would be out of sight when they arrived, but Sergeant Sombat had arranged for two undercover officers to be loitering in front of the Soi 11 entrance way to the alley, on the lookout for men selling drugs. They would have an arrest tonight.

CHAPTER THIRTY-THREE

Matt was relieved when John's call came.

"Hey man, what's going on? You had me worried. Did you have to break out of jail?"

"Ahhh, sort of. Let's just say we won't be getting any help from my special forces friends. We need to meet up. We can discuss the details then. Where are you?"

"Neung's guys have me stashed in a safehouse somewhere in town. On the north side. I'm not quite sure exactly where."

"Well I don't want to involve them any further. I've talked to Neung and he has given me some new information. We'll keep him out of this. His political exposure is way too high already. Have his guys get your 4Runner. I'll send you the coordinates where we should meet."

"Okay but one thing you should know something came up in Bangkok and Jade had to go back and deal with it. For right now it's just you and me."

"Well we'll have to get along without her though she has some skills we could use. Right now we need to find some friends here and make some plans quick. I think we may be running out of time with regard to this mad monk."

"Okay. I'm on my way."

The coordinates that John sent Matt led a further forty kilometers

126

south, towards the Malaysian border and several hundred meters off the coastal road, along a rough dirt track into the forest. Matt found two large thatched-roof native huts hidden in a small clearing under the dark shadows of the surrounding trees. There was a motorbike and two 4x4s parked to the side facing out back down the entry road. An electric generator was humming behind the huts. Matt backed into a space alongside the 4x4s.

As he walked toward the two houses John came to the door of the larger one and waved him in.

"Come on in. I've got some people I want you to meet."

Matt looked over the inside of the house as he walked in. It was bare bamboo walls with water stains. No real furnishings except for a fan standing in the corner, a small table and a few extra chairs to the side. A couple of cots sat alongside the wall with mosquito netting draped over them. There was mildew on the ceiling. A kitchen space was behind the entry room but that seemed to be somewhat sparsely set up also. Matt thought, maybe this is the back woods version of a safe house.

There were two uniformed officers sitting in chairs around the table with a map spread across it. Another chair was pulled back where John had been sitting.

"These are two friends of mine from years back when I was an advisor to the Border Patrol Police. Colonel Unpakorn and Sgt. Major Tala. Unlike my special forces colleagues, they carry a sense of obligation to old friends."

Matt greeted the two men and sat down at the table as John directed.

"These are men and an organization I know we can trust. When I called they had already received a heads up that we had a problem. Was that from you?"

"Indirectly I guess. I got in touch with Sgt. Major Chatri, an army friend who has worked with them before. He said he would talk to some of the people he knew who were stationed down here."

Matt nodded towards the map laid out on the table.

"I see plans are being made. What are we going to do?"

John smiled. "We're going to squeeze these pseudo religious bastards who are using this hidden temple as a base. Let me show you what we've got in mind."

John leaned over the map which showed the temple site and the entrance road.

"We'll do a two-sided assault on the temple. A platoon of the Border Patrol Police will make a very noisy early morning assault along the road leading to the front entrance to the temple. However, they will hold back prior to entry to give us a chance to see what rats might run out the back. Our mission is to come in from the hills to the back of the temple which has an opening leading to the helicopter pad. The head monk will probably be hustled out that way. We'll intercept him and any hostages they may bring along."

"When do we go?"

"Tomorrow night. We get in place on the hill overlooking the temple. We move down and hit them at 5 a.m. just as the Border Patrol Police on the road start their action. That should cause the maximum confusion and give us an opportunity."

After John showed the Thai officers out, he came back in and sat down next to Matt, paused for a moment and then put a hand on Matt's arm.

"There is something I need to talk to you about."

Matt just nodded.

John, whose manner had been brisk, very much in charge, now slumped back into his chair. War spares no one, even the supposed victors. John was evidence of that. The deep marks on John's face, left by the violence he had faced in years of warfare, seemed to Matt to have deepened. John looked at the maps and then across the room for a minute before he spoke. His voice one of resignation.

"This is my last rodeo, partner. I don't belong out here anymore. I've lost more than a step or two but more importantly, I killed a guy who was nothing more than a kid the other day. He was after me with my death on his mind so I can say to myself I was justified, but I can't be responsible for taking more lives. I've taken too many down the years. Maybe I've been living with the buddhists too long, but I don't think my karma can handle any more killing."

Matt had never seen John this despondent but in a way he wasn't surprised. He himself still carried strong memories of his past shooting scrapes and killings himself. They had all been necessary in the combat context, but he understood what John was saying about the burden of carrying memories of the killings. Not all of the wounds suffered nor scars carried by combat soldiers were visible.

"I understand that. What are you going to do now?"

"I'm on for tomorrow night. I failed to find Jack's daughter for him but she wasn't the only one. There are more girls in there and I'll finish what I started. After this I'm a desk warrior. I'll give all the advice and contacts you and Jade want, but I'd be a burden out in the field."

"You're still one of the best."

"No more. Maybe I was one of the best long ago but I can't keep up physically or mentally anymore. Also, and you are one of the people who should understand, I'm carrying too many memories. I'm surrounded by ghosts. When you get older Matt you stop focusing on the future and the past crowds in."

"I know that feeling. Well than let's make this raid a grand sendoff. Let's take these guys down."

John nodded in agreement. "Yeah, let's put this monk and his sex slave ring out of business."

He went on, "One thing though. I talked with Jade and told her the plan and that we were going in without her. She's not happy but I don't feel we can wait for her."

Matt, who was still unsure of Jade's value in combat, nodded. "That's okay. She'll just have to live with it. We've got a job to do."

***

Jade was pissed. The phone call with John telling her not to bother coming down south, as they would have things wrapped up before she could get there, was not what she wanted to hear.

She was used to men and their misguided attempts to keep her from the action. It had been the bane of her military career and one of the main reasons she had opted out of the army.

Well she had ways and means that neither John nor Matt were aware of. They would be surprised but she would be in on the action come hell or high water. She started to make calls to some of her former U.S. military friends living and working in Thailand.

CHAPTER THIRTY-FOUR

The next day John and Matt were joined at the forest hut by a Sgt. Somit of the Border Patrol Police. He told them his job was to guide them to the starting point at the hill formation behind the temple and assist them throughout. He had with him a Motorola SRX 2200 tactical radio with which he could keep contact with the BP troops at the front of the temple. He was also carrying a Rocket Propelled Grenade launcher (RPG) along with his regular issue M4 carbine. He also had two M4s for Matt and John and extra magazines. When Matt asked what the RPG was for, the Sergeant answered, "Just in case."

It had rained during the day and the air was still hot and thick with tropical steam as they rode out to the base of the hill behind the temple. The climb up to the initial observation point on the jungle hilltop was steep and slippery. John was having trouble, breathing heavily, moving slowly, and grabbing at branches as he went along. Matt led the way up. Sgt. Somit moved along easily. All three were drenched in sweat when they stopped on top to observe the temple and catch their breath.

After midnight they eased down the hillside to a closer observation position. They would wait there until the noise making attack was launched at the front of the temple. Sgt. Somit said his commanding officer was concerned that in the confusion and dim early morning light his troops might mistake Matt and John as a threat. Sgt. Somit was known to the troops who would be coming into the temple from the opposite side. He was to lead the way to insure no shooting mistakes were made.

There were no sounds or movement in the jungle surrounding them except for the slow dripping of rain from the trees drenched during the day. They were covered with mud from the controlled slide down the hill. From their new position, on the lower hill side, they could clearly see the temple below them, outlined by several lights which had been kept burning though the night. There was no movement. Whatever guards had been posted were sleeping or not bothering to walk their posts. There was a chopper sitting on the helipad but no lights or activity around it.

John was scanning the temple area with night vision binoculars, a U.S. army PVS-14 model which Sgt. Somit had brought along from the Border Patrol supplies.

John leaned over and gave Matt and then Sgt. Somit a look through the binoculars.

"No movement. No sign of surveillance. I guess we're going to be their morning wake up call. Let's move down to the edge of the clearing. We'll need to be in position and move quickly once the BP guys start the noise."

Though no activity showed outside the temple there was movement inside. The girls, still in their rooms, had been given an early wake up call. They were to be up and ready to go at sunrise. No explanation was given but they were going to take a helicopter ride.

Leung Somboon knew the time had come. This jungle temple had served its purpose. He would leave a staff here to continue the very profitable business of transferring young women to what he referred to as their 'new homes.' When the inevitable raid came he would be far away.

Leung Somboon had made his calls to followers in differing countries. His eventual destination would be the South of

France but, for the moment, he had been offered a safe haven within Asia. He already had a base of operations there and his people had located a very private property in an area near to an important customer base of the ultra-wealthy. He would have time to plan his future steps away from the interference of the generals in Thailand.

CHAPTER THIRTY-FIVE

The silence of the night was slowly disappearing. The birds in the trees surrounding them began their pre sunrise chorus of greetings. The slow dripping of rain from the trees had stopped. The 5 a.m. starting time had come and gone. John was fixed on his watch and muttering to himself. Matt just let it go. This wasn't a Ranger operation so he expected some miscues. The Border Patrol Police may have had trouble getting into position due to the need to maintain silence. It was better to be a few minutes late than to lose the advantage of surprise.

However, they could now see some movement within the temple grounds. Some lights had come on. Things were definitely stirring. John asked, "Do we wait on them or start moving?"

Matt said, "We wait. It would be embarrassing if we were the only ones assaulting the temple."

Sgt. Somit didn't seem worried. "They will move soon. Be patient."

A few more minutes went by. The sun, rising over the hills behind them, was starting to show the first signs of dawn light on the hill top across the valley. It was a jungle night shade gently being lifted. They saw figures moving behind the temple but couldn't make out what they were doing.

Suddenly there was the sound of automatic weapons fire on the other side of the temple. Then there were a couple of explosions that Matt identified as hand grenade explosions.

Sgt. Somit was already rising to move down the last bit of muddy hillside and across the rice paddy. Matt turned to John, "Let's go soldier."

John nodded and then smiling at Matt and extending his hand in invitation towards the temple said, "I understand that Rangers lead the way."

Shafts of early morning sun light from behind them were reaching the floor of the valley they were facing.

Sgt. Somit and Matt led the move down the final bit of hillside and began the balanced half run along the rice paddy dykes towards the temple. Matt heard a shout behind him. John was down, sitting in the muddy water of the rice paddy holding his chest. Matt stopped and turned back. Running to John, Matt yelled to Sgt. Somit to let him know there was a problem. Sgt. Somit stopped and watched Matt going to John.

John was very pale and breathing with difficulty.

Matt leaned over him. He was looking for a wound. Had John somehow been shot by a temple guard?

"What's wrong? Have you been hit?"

John shook his head.

"I think it's my heart. I had a strong pain and can't breathe."

Matt sunk down beside John and began to lift him up. He decided they would have to carry John to the temple. He turned to Sgt. Somit who was now walking back towards them carrying the RPG on his shoulder. Behind Sgt. Somit Matt could see activity on the chopper pad. The turbine engine was started and the blades were starting to rotate. Several figures, one in a saffron robe, ran out the back of the temple toward the chopper. They were losing the chance to catch the head monk.

Sgt. Somit was now next to John and Matt. He turned and saw what Matt was seeing, the escape of the temple leaders they were trying to capture. Sgt. Somit raised the RPG aiming towards the chopper.

Matt yelled, "No, don't shoot. There may be captives with them."

Sgt. Somit looked back towards Matt and said, "Orders are to stop them no matter what." He turned towards the temple again, raising the RPG to an aiming position on his shoulder. Matt jumped up and hit Sgt. Somit's shoulder as he fired. The round went off target hitting the temple wall.

Matt was furious.

"No. We can't take a chance on killing civilians. Now come and help me with John."

The turbine engines on the chopper were winding to a higher pitch. It would soon have the rpms to lift off and escape.

Then Matt heard another chopper thumping overhead and a voice speaking English came over Sgt. Somit's tactical radio. He was surprised, looked at Matt and then extended the radio to him.

It was Jade. "Hey boys, I'm up above. Do you need some help?"

The chopper on the temple helipad, lifted off, nose down, heading across the rice paddies, further up the valley, and gaining speed to elevate higher and leave the scene.

Jade yelled through the radio. "It looks like the bad guys may be getting away. Do you want me to follow them and find out where they set down?"

Even though Jade couldn't see him do it, Matt shook his head.

"No, leave them go. We got a problem with John. I think he's had a heart attack. Set down on the temple's helipad. We'll bring John to you. We need to get him to a good hospital quick."

There were a few seconds of silence then Jade answered. "Roger that. The guy in the other seat suggests we take him up to Hat Yai. There is a hospital there with a helipad. It's used by the offshore oil field workers when they have a problem. Setting down."

Then a new problem arose. Matt could hear the familiar sound of the buzz of automatic rifle rounds flying through the air around them. The RPG explosion had alerted some guards within the temple to their presence. Two figures had appeared in the door of the temple and started shooting at them across the rice paddy.

John was very pale and not talking. Matt yelled to Sgt. Somit to cover them as he lifted John in a fireman's carry.

Sgt. Somit fired back into the temple doorway hitting one of the guards. The other disappeared inside the temple, possibly not worried about them now that the head monk had escaped.

When they got to the helipad the chopper Jade was piloting had set down. A Thai crewman opened the side door to help Matt load John inside. Jade was in her seat looking out at them through the side windshield which she had opened. Matt could see the concern and stress on her face.

Sgt. Somit moved to the temple door providing cover for the helipad.

Matt moved up next to the window and yelled to her. "Glad you're here. John needs medical attention quick."

Jade gave him a thumbs up as the rotor blades whined with increased rpms. "Get out of the way. We're going."

He quickly backed away. "Take care of him."

Jade nodded as the chopper began to lift off. She held her hand in the phone position, thumb at her ear and little finger extended to let Matt know she would call to give him a report on John.

Matt backed off and turned towards the doorway leading into the temple. Hopefully something inside would help to make them feel better about losing the cult leaders and the possible captives they took with them.

The sun had now fully risen, twenty miles to the east, out on the Gulf of Thailand. The helicopter pilot flew directly into its glare. The ocean was calm and flat. A large ocean-going yacht maneuvered to a position heading slowly into the northeast wind. The helicopter turned, flared up and settled on the chopper pad on the stern of the ship. It was just a touch and go, a drop off of Leung Somboon's group from the temple. His temporary residence in a nearby country had been arranged. It was one in which the Thai generals would be hard pressed to follow him. It also had the advantage of being located near to several of his best ultra-wealthy clients, all of whom had excellent security arrangements.

All the same, Leung Somboon was not completely relieved. It was clear from the rocket explosion near his helicopter that the attackers had intended to kill him. That puzzled him. His value to the junta would be great if they could capture him and have a show trial exposing him and discrediting him before the nation. His death would only inflame his legion of followers who would direct their anger against the junta. Who was it who wanted him dead? In any case he now had time to think about it. He would gather information and see how he could expand his power further. First he would reassure his followers that he was alive and continuing his religious mission.

CHAPTER THIRTY-SIX

Noi wasn't sure at first what to do with the information Plato had found. Normally she would defer to Matt on anything having to do with one of his cases but Matt was down south. She never called when he was busy on a case, rather she waited for him to check in. At the same time, she felt that getting this information to someone quickly might be important so she thought of Neung. She had Plato give her screen shots of the site he had brought up and called Neung immediately.

Neung was excited, or as excited as his professional status allowed him to be. He needed to look in depth at what Plato had come up with.

"Noi, this is great. I want to arrange a meeting with you and Plato."

Over at his desk, still playing with the site he had found, Plato was watching Noi. When she looked over at him he understood immediately that there was a danger of him being brought to the center stage. He shook his head 'no.'

"I don't think Plato wants to be involved more. He is happy being in the background."

"Noi, he is probably the only one of us who really knows how to navigate behind the curtains of the dark web without being detected. I will keep his identity hidden but I need him to help me understand what is possible and what is not now that he has hacked their site."

"Okay. I'll talk to him but we should meet in a very discrete place."

"I'll make the arrangements. We should do this tonight. He should bring his computer to walk me through what he found, okay?"

"Okay, let me know where and when."

Neung had thought the importance and need for security of the discussion of Plato's cyber findings merited continuing to use one of the DSI's safe houses. He certainly wasn't ready to have his boss or office spies looking over his shoulder as he shaped the information. He arranged to have Noi and Plato picked up and brought to the house.

Noi wanted to make Plato comfortable. When she and Plato arrived, after introducing Plato to Neung, she spoke to that immediately.

"We ask that you don't identify either of us by name or company. If you have to answer questions about your source could you just identify us as independent computer consultants?"

Neung was not surprised. It was the classic 'no identification of sources or means' intelligence reporting guideline. He said yes though he was unsure he could keep his promise.

"I'll do as you ask, but I need you both to commit to following this up. I need to show my bosses commitment if we expect DSI to take this further."

What he didn't say was that until he was sure which way the political winds were blowing within his agency and then within the military junta, he didn't want to bring the dark web finding to light.

Noi nodded and said, "Matt asked us to look at this site. I'll be more comfortable when he's here."

"I spoke with him. I couldn't give him any detailed information over the phone but he's on his way back from the south right now. We can brief him tomorrow."

Then looking to Plato he asked for a deeper explanation.

"I have to understand just what you found. Is it possible to turn the website in some way? Just observing or capturing the person running the site is not enough. That person is acting on behalf of others."

Noi nodded to Plato. "Give him what we have."

CHAPTER THIRTY-SEVEN

The hospital at Hat Yai was a three-story building with a full medical staff and it had a cardiology department. Jade and her 'borrowed' chopper were able to get John to the hospital well within the 'Golden Hour', the standard for saving heart attack patients. The quick evacuation saved John's life.

When Matt arrived after his frantic two-hour drive up from the southern border area, Jade was standing in the brightly lit and aseptic corridor outside the intensive care unit of the hospital. His first question was, "How is John?"

"He's going to make it. We got him here in time. The doc doesn't want us to try and talk to him right now. He's been given some pretty strong medicine and is dozing. They said when he's awake and stabilized, we can see him. They emphasized, no stress. Keep him calm and give him some time to recover."

Matt's shoulders sagged in relief. He walked over to a nearby bench and sat down. He waved at Jade inviting her to sit next to him.

He looked straight at her and nodded to her. "I apologize. I will never question your abilities again."

Then he paused and looked at her with new respect. "How did you get down here in time to follow up the raid, and where did the chopper come from?"

Jade wasn't about to let Matt go with just a few words of apology, but she decided now was not the time to rub salt into

142

the wounds. Their shared concern about John was the important issue at the moment.

"Not all that hard if you have the right skills and know the right people. I have a number of ex-military friends who work with Thai aviation companies, piloting choppers, taking men and supplies out to the drilling platforms in the Gulf of Thailand. I got in touch with one who was scheduled to test out a chopper that had just been serviced. Luckily he was another adrenalin junkie I knew from Iraq and not too concerned about being involved in your raid from the air view. He agreed I could fly second seat in the test run. We made a date to meet, just a short flight up the coast from the temple. I was able to fly in last night, met with him and we took off at O dark thirty before the raid. I thought we would be late but it seems you were behind schedule. I saw some figures escape on that chopper. Did you get anything good inside? Any of the girls?"

"Yeah, we at least spooked a few of the top guys to run without taking along two girls they were holding captive. We were just in time for them. They had been told to be ready for an early morning departure. Our raid stopped that. So some good came out of it. The Border Patrol Police are going over the place finding a lot of interesting things: a TV studio, modern medical and surgical facilities and a lot of weapons. The soldiers or monks inside didn't put up a real fight. It seemed when their leader got away they felt their duty was done."

"What happened to the girls?"

"They are both from Bangkok and will be going up there to be debriefed pretty soon. They were both somewhat hysterical, crying with relief to be out of there."

"I'm not complaining since it allowed me to get there in time, but why the late start to the raid?"

"The Border Patrol Police were late in starting the distraction in front of the temple, so we had to sit by until the sun was coming up. I think we still could have stopped the leaders at the temple from getting into their chopper and getting away. Then

John went down and he became the first priority. We had them in our hands, dammit."

"After the chopper lifted off it took a straight line out to the gulf. They may have had a landing point out on the water. Maybe we can track that."

Matt was not about to doubt Jade any more but had to ask.

"What are the points he could go to in the gulf? Wouldn't an oil platform or an island be pretty much a dead end?"

"Let me ask some of my friends who fly over the gulf all the time. They might have some ideas."

"Okay. I need some sleep. After we are sure John is stabilized why don't we plan to go up to Bangkok. We can talk through all the details on the way. Later on we can find out what the girls have to say to the police and then we can give Neung a briefing."

CHAPTER THIRTY-EIGHT

A few hours later, after a brief talk with John, who was still dazed from the meds, they started back to Bangkok.

Matt found the long ride back interesting. Whether it was his apology or the post-action let down motivating her, Jade had opened up a bit and talked to him about her background. As had Matt, she grew up without a father. Living on the south side of Chicago, she helped to care for her younger brother and tried to back stop her single mom on all the house needs, starting to work from age thirteen. Jade won a scholarship to a leading prep school. She had done well there and managed to get an appointment to West Point. When Matt asked about her time in the service, she told him she loved the flying and the community ethos, but had become unhappy with what she termed the Green Machine's obsession with public relations practices and the fixation of most officers with their climb up the promotion ladder. Those were views Matt shared, and the talk gave them a bit more understanding of each other.

Then Matt remembered the reason for her trip back to Bangkok.

"How is Apple? Is she going to be okay?"

"It's going to take a while for the physical bruises to heal. I'm not sure how long the psychological bruises will take."

"Did you find out who beat her up?"

"Yeah. I found out. The guy won't be beating up any more

women for some time."

Matt glanced over at her. Jade was just staring ahead, looking out the windshield.

"Something you want to tell me?"

"Not now. Another time, after we check up on Apple."

When they finally got to Bangkok, Matt dropped her off at her apartment and went back to his place.

He didn't call Noi when he arrived back but sent her a message that he was back, safe but exhausted. He told her that he would crash at his apartment and call her in the morning.

Matt was still sleeping when his phone rang in the morning. It wasn't Noi, but Neung.

"Hey Matt, are you awake?'

"I am now. What's up?

"We had a meeting yesterday with Noi, and one of her computer guys. I think we need to repeat that meeting today."

"I thought the problem was solved. We put the temple out of business and got the girls back."

"Matt, it's good you don't have to survive in my world. I need to present information on this dark website and its activities to my politically-oriented management. I'm counting on Noi, her computer guy, and you to give me the background to help me understand what it's practical to do. I'm not sure this government wants to be embarrassed into taking public actions they would rather keep under the covers, as you say."

"Actually we say undercover, but I understand. Send me the directions to the meeting place and I'll be there. I'll bring Noi and her guy along."

CHAPTER THIRTY-NINE

Neung used the same safe house as before for the follow-up meeting. He had spoken with Len LeBlanc and had promised he would share any information or decisions that might be of interest to Interpol. Len had agreed to stand by until he learned how Neung's agency and the Thai government wanted to proceed.

When Matt, Noi and Plato arrived it could be seen that Plato was nervous. The previous day had been one more meeting than he wanted, however Noi, who he worshipped, had reminded him that they had agreed with Neung to see this through.

After the greetings, Matt asked to be brought up to date on the previous day's meeting.

"Are we finished or do we keep going after this guy and his cult?"

Neung nodded to Noi and Plato, "Actually I need Noi and Plato to hear my take on yesterday because some of it was familiar to me and a lot was new. Then we can discuss the possibilities."

He continued. "I believe that this kidnapping and slavery business is just one part of what is happening here and the rest is over my political head. We've learned a lot thanks to Plato successfully hacking the dark website the monks are using."

Matt saw Plato wince at this open mention of his hacking.

Neung looked to Noi and Plato.

"The real question is who is behind the site? Can we identify the location? If it isn't here in Thailand, where are the website's servers located? Can we track them and get to the organizing force behind this ring?"

Noi looked at Plato. She and Plato had discussed the possibilities late into the night. Plato had done further work looking into the site, but it was obvious he wasn't about to speak to anyone but her so it was up to her to summarize.

"Actually we can find the location of the guy doing the web work here, due his careless mistake. He seems to be Thai and he's located here in Bangkok. However, I don't think that's the answer you're looking for. There are multiple servers being used. We tried to zero in, but if you ask for the usual list of suspects in terms of major actors, then it gets complicated."

Noi looked over at Matt, "We agreed when we went back to the office yesterday Plato and I would look to see what other actors were involved."

Matt asked her, "What do you mean by other actors?"

"It is probable that what we found, the identity of this one operator, is just the surface of the organization. It may be that state actors were backstopping this site, both for money and as a way of destabilizing Thailand politically. There has been evidence of North Korean action here for example. The North Koreans have initiated multiple efforts to earn hard currency to overcome the effects of the international trade sanctions against their nuclear program. They duped the Bank of Bangladesh out of $81 million. More recently they have created and marketed a new bitcoin product, Hold Coin, through the dark web, defrauding bitcoin holders out of over $500 million dollars."

Matt raised his eyebrows, "Wow, that's not small change."

Neung picked it up.

"That's not all, as Noi said, they have multiple programs going, but have sited the external effort overseas. For instance, the North Korean blackmail effort hacking Sony and inserting malware a couple of years ago supposedly originated from the St. Regis hotel here in town. However, that was just the launching point, through some agent's laptop. The program itself was found to be North Korean in origin."

Here Neung paused.

Matt was sitting back in his seat, more than a bit stunned at the magnitude of what Noi and Plato had come up with.

"That leaves us out of the next steps doesn't it? We're not equipped to chase a guy who is under the protection of a rogue nation."

Matt turned to Noi, "Have you any, best possible, ideas on the location of the server used by the web site?"

Noi nodded, "That's another problem. It seems probable the originating server is located in Chinese territory, specifically the Chinese Special Administrative Region of Macau."

"So this is a Chinese activity?"

Neung stepped in, "That's not clear. It gets more complicated. The recent history of the North Koreans is that they have a record of routing their dark web activities through China. That acts as a firebreak for them. The North Koreans have had a presence in Macau for more than twenty years often using Triad contacts to advance their interests. The Chinese may be allowing it as a form of support for Kim, Jong-Un. The U.S. and other western nations are hesitant to launch a cyber-attack against the North Korean operations as they fear China may take that action as one aimed against them. The North Koreans have excellent cover."

"So you see Matt, I have to turn this over to the political levels here. I will share some information with Interpol to pay them back for starting us in the right direction. The full portfolio will go to my superiors. As bad as they want this monk caught, upsetting China is beyond the realm of possibility."

Matt shrugged his shoulders, "I hate to see him get away but it's beyond us now isn't it?"

"Yeah, I'll let you know what feedback I get but any further action will have to be sanctioned by a higher power."

"Okay we'll stand by and wait to hear from you."

CHAPTER FORTY

Leung Somboon watched from the deck of the yacht as it moved closer to the shore to drop anchor. The overnight voyage had taken over thirty hours. He was sick of the ocean and tired of the constraints of the yacht. He brooded over the attempt to kill him. The generals had shown that they now preferred him dead. He needed the sanctuary of Macao.

Ahead of the boat there was a pier sited on the waterfront below a large villa. The villa grounds were extensive and were surrounded by a security fence on all sides leading down to the water. A motorboat came out from the shore and was secured alongside the yacht so the passengers could disembark.

When they walked up to the pier from the floating gangway, Leung Somboon was greeted by a rotund older Chinese man. He was dressed informally in a short sleeved white shirt hanging over his belt and khaki slacks and wearing flip flops. Above him on the sloping grounds of the path up to the villas were two watchful men, each holding an automatic weapon.

The Chinese man nodded to the monk, smiling and showing large white front teeth, and greeted him in Cantonese dialect Chinese. Leung Somboon responded in kind. The man, Won, Kuok-Koi, known as "Broken Tooth Won" from a past auto crash, during a gang related shoot-out, was the boss of the 14 K Triad. His repaired smile had cost substantial money and only served to remind people of his violent past.

Starting as a parentless teen in a Macao border refugee camp, he had fought his way into bottom level membership in the 14 K gang. He then quickly rose to the top by exhibiting an ability for violence unusual even for a triad. Won's organization was both a supplier and a key customer for Leung Somboon's criminal activities. The villa would be the new center of the monk's operations until it was convenient for him and his aides to move to Europe.

The villa served as both the host's living quarters and offices. The server Plato had tracked around the world was based here, under the sub rosa protection of the Chinese military and civil government that administered Macao.

Leung Somboon turned and gestured to the three aides who had followed behind to join him. They hurried up the gangway to the dock along with the two young women they had brought with them from the temple. The women were, in essence, a form of currency that Leung Somboon could use to repay his hosts for their assistance.

CHAPTER FORTY-ONE

One of the rituals that Noi and Matt went through when he came back from chasing down one case or another was the reunion ritual. While he was in Bangkok they had developed a form of relaxed time sharing, both respecting that they needed to give the other time and space for whatever work or social demands came up. The exception was the reunion. They both felt it was a necessary time to reignite their bond. It had been a night relieved of the tensions they had both been under. Noi had stayed over at Matt's place. In the morning, not too early, they were ready to go back to their normal schedule.

After Noi left to go to her office Matt decided he should do the same thing. He had a business office in the Emporium Tower in a central area of Bangkok with a shared receptionist. It was an upmarket location that his mother, active in Bangkok real estate for years, had negotiated for him and insisted he use. She accepted Matt's casual attitude towards his employment as an on again off again training consultant to the Thai government departments of forestry and national parks, but she said he had to have an office, not work from home. It was a 'face' thing for her. His unofficial security work and sometime partnership with Neung and the DSI was something he didn't share with her.

Matt was looking forward to some casual time. Maybe later he would go and shoot some pool. There was only one thing better to relax him and that mission had already been accomplished.

He made a call to the hospital to check on John and they told him that John was doing well, resting, and under observation for a few more days. The hospital staffer he talked with said she would give John the message that Matt had called.

Matt didn't have to wait long. As he knew would happen, John found a way to call him once he got the message.

John sounded strong.

"Matt, I'm sorry. I let you down on the raid. I knew I was slowing down but I'm definitely a desk jockey after this."

"Just take care of your health. Recover first. Then think about what you might want to do."

"Thanks buddy. I'll work on the recovery part, but my future path is pretty clear. Thanks for carrying me out of that rice paddy." Laughs, "I always knew a rice paddy would get me."

"When are we going to see you back up here in Bangkok? Do you have an ETA yet?"

"They're telling me another night must be spent here. Then I've got a driver from the law firm who will take me back home. I'll let you know."

"Okay old soldier. Glad you're feeling better. Call me anytime. The big man got away from us, but we managed to rescue two girls who were being held in the temple."

"Good. Talk later."

Matt hung up and thought about how relieved he was. John meant a lot to him. John had been his mentor since he came home to Bangkok, carrying a burden of post combat anger and drinking too much. Having him out of the action was definitely a setback.

Matt was thinking about calling Jade to check on Apple's status. Before he could call, his phone rang with a call from Neung.

"Hey Matt, have you had a chance to relax?"

"Yeah, I'm doing good, just sitting in my office trying to think what should be next."

"Well I don't want to disturb you but we've got some additional information on the raid I thought you would want."

"Okay, hit me."

"It's not good news. They got the two girls up to Bangkok now. They have settled down and we were able to debrief them. Unfortunately, they asked about the other two girls."

"What other two girls? There were more girls in the temple than the two we brought out?"

"It seems so. They must have been in the group on the chopper that got away."

"Awww hell, what does this mean? Are you still going after the monk then?"

"It's not so simple. Now it's international. There are some meetings going on to decide what to do. I should tell you the top government people here are much more concerned about the mastermind behind the dark web site we found and the international connections, than the girls. I'll let you know what decisions are made. There is nothing for you to do now. Just standby and I'll get back to you."

"Okay. Let me know what's decided when you can."

Matt hung up and sat back shaking his head. If he and Sgt. Somit had been able to hustle over to the chopper maybe they would have been able to stop it and get the girls free as well as stopping the mad monk from escaping. He wasn't going to tell John until later. It would upset him too much.

CHAPTER FORTY-TWO

Far to the north, outside of Chiang Mai, Major General Preecha had returned to his mountain villa for a rest and a break from the heat of the south. After the raid on the temple his officer charged with keeping an eye on the temple and its operations had reported to him. He knew the head monk had escaped but not where he had gone.

He hadn't expected visitors but a house servant came to him and said he had a phone call from a foreign man who could speak Thai but would only identify himself as Robert.

The general laughed and agreed to take the call.

"Hi Robert, I should have known you would be in touch. Your firm follows up on things quite quickly. I presume you would like to talk."

"Good evening General, yes I would like to talk and I'm nearby. Would you mind if I came over? This should be a quiet talk."

"Of course, come now and I'll have a cold beer for you. Not the Thai way I promise. No ice cubes."

Robert was the general's contact from the American embassy. He was the CIA agent tasked with handling the relationship with the general. Inside the Bangkok station the general was just known as 'the tiger' or in classified communications as WU-Tiger with the two-letter identifier of the operation listed first. Many of the agency's sources within the Thai military had years before been given the code names of wildlife to be found in Thailand. The current general heading the junta had been WU-Buffalo when contracted in prior years. It was an inside joke by his original recruiter as he hadn't considered the young military officer very bright though he held a key position at the time. The buffalo surprised all his handlers by consistently being in the right place at the right time. He became one of the three generals to advance to a power sharing agreement at the top during the last coup. He had forsaken the agency contacts many years before as being of no use to him.

General Preecha, or WU-Tiger, had been a consistent source of value since his drug smuggling days in Laos years before. Now, having been shunted outside the junta, the agency considered him a valuable source on potential opposition from other military groups to the generals in power.

For his part, the fact that the agency still came to him for information made the general feel he was still important and somewhat soothed his anger at being excluded from the cabal in power in Bangkok. He no longer needed money from the agency. He had profited greatly from the drug trade over the years. His payment from his 'handlers' would consist of favors, often just promising to overlook certain of his drug activities over the years or, most recently, insuring a study visa to the U.S for his youngest daughter and facilitating her acceptance into USC.

Robert sat down opposite the general in his open study area. Though the night was cool, the general used an old-style ceiling fan in each room to slowly circulate the air. The interior walls were bamboo with a large window on one wall with a screen opening to the night air. The general had a fondness for Chinese art, especially nature drawings, some were hundreds of years old. Several of these art pieces decorated the wall of the room.

Robert opened with his usual series of banal questions concerning the general's well-being. He made a point of asking how the youngest daughter, Pare, was doing at USC.

The general replied, "I'm doing well Robert and Pare is doing very well, thank you. She's enjoying the USC culture, possibly too much, but I let her mother look after that. What concerns you this evening?"

Robert smiled, it was always easy doing business with the general as he was much more open to directness in conversation than many Thai.

"There has been some military activity in the south concerning our entrepreneurial Buddhist monk. Is there anything you can tell me about that? We heard that there were some Americans involved."

"You know one of the Americans, it was John Scales, the former Special Forces man. I was surprised to see him down there. I heard he was working with a law firm in Bangkok."

One of Robert's fellow spooks at the embassy kept up a casual relationship with John as he had been a long-time source and was considered an expert on the Thai scene.

"I've heard of John. What was he up to? I would think he's a bit old for field work."

The general laughed, "Be careful Robert, you'll insult me, remember I'm older than John. You're right I was surprised to see him there. We've been friends for many years going back to the days in Laos. He told me he was going to the south trying to find some rich young girls who had been kidnapped from Bangkok. He was looking into a possible hideout where the girls might be held. I understood he was acting on behalf of a friend in Bangkok. Unfortunately, it didn't end well for John. First he barely escaped an attempted assassination attempt at his hotel. Then I heard he had a heart attack and ended up in the hospital."

"Did he find the girls?"

"John joined a raid on the temple where the girls had been hidden. Apparently there were two other Americans working with him. I understand two girls were rescued but the head monk escaped by helicopter."

"Can I ask how you were involved?"

The general tilted his head slightly. This was his tell. Time to dance a bit.

"My troops do some security work in the south."

The general decided it was time to turn the questions back to his agency friend.

"What is the interest of your firm in this?"

Robert paused a bit longer than usual, it was his tell that he would be hiding something, but the general expected nothing less.

"Well, it seems the monk's money-making activities were focused though the use of a site on the dark web. Sources have shared with us that this site had international support. Just who or what country the international operators are, still has to be determined. We're interested in any information that will help in tracking that down."

"If you're hoping I can help you with that I'm afraid I'll have to disappoint you. My unit's relationship with the monk was an arm's length relationship, focused solely on security advice."

Robert put down his beer. "Okay, thanks, you understand, we just had to check."

"I understand. I'm sure your firm has the ability to handle the international end of this."

Robert had started to rise to leave, but the general paused for a moment holding up his hand. Robert stopped and watched him.

"I can say this. There was something that struck me as somewhat strange about a possible transaction with the monk. The monk and his group seem to have great resources. He offered to pay a million dollars for my men to train some of his followers and provide security assistance."

Robert settled back in his chair. "So the monk has a lot of money."

"Yes and also a lot of differing types of money."

"What do you mean by that?"

"Well he gave me a choice. He also said he could provide something called bitcoins to the value of two million dollars. I know nothing of bitcoins. I had to turn him down."

"Thank you, that's interesting. I believe it will be useful."

ACT III
CHAPTER FORTY-THREE

It was early evening. As the sun's light dimmed in Benjasiri park outside his office, Matt felt he had to get out. Several days had passed and there had been no word from Neung. He decided to go to the park. As he entered, he walked past the tai chi group which worked out each night. Further down the walkway he found a quiet place to sit down on a bench near the lake. The subdued park lights were on and the trees cast long shadows over the lawn. The cooler evening air and emergence of oriental exercise groups such as the tai chi club gave a sense of peace to the park. He always found it calming to watch the joggers running on the path which looped around the small lake. He sat and brooded on his failure.

It had not been his job alone to find Jack's daughter. John was already on the case. He had found John, but he felt a sense of failure that they hadn't been able to save the girl. He hadn't seen Jack yet. The army had given permission for the release of the body for a cremation ceremony and delegated an officer from the Lumpini district police to tell Jack. He had heard that Jack was devastated by the death of his daughter. The involvement of the monks had not been mentioned. The cover story was that she had drown near the holiday island of Koh Samui while on an impromptu holiday. It had been made clear to Jack that it was in his interest to go along with the story. The three-day ceremony at Wat That Thong, which specialized in funeral cremations and ceremonies, would start tomorrow evening. Matt was obligated to go but was dreading it. Jack had learned that when the kidnappers had ordered him to stop the search in exchange for a promise to get his daughter back, she was already dead.

Closing down the temple and saving two of the kidnapped girls was some solace, but they hadn't gotten the monk in charge or the other girls. Matt was left feeling very dissatisfied.

It was then that Matt's mobile phone rang. It was Neung and he was very brief. "Where are you? I understand you're not in your office."

"I'm sitting in the park trying to get over my failure."

"I don't know what failure you're talking about but stay there. Someone will be coming to talk to you."

"What someone? Neung, I'm in no mood to talk to anyone."

It was too late, Neung had hung up. Matt had no choice but to wait.

The park would close at 8 p.m. It was growing dark. The shadows from the trees extended further out over the small lake. There were fewer people around as the flow of the workout crowd ebbed. The multicolored lights in the fountain within the lake were providing a kaleidoscoptic show. It was a familiar and normally a relaxing scene for Matt, but he was growing impatient with waiting.

In the shadows under the trees, down the walking path, there was a figure approaching.

In the dark Matt couldn't make out any features except that it was a tall, well-built male.

"Hey Matt, are you meditating?"

Matt relaxed. "Well, yes, I was expecting the unexpected and here you are. How are you doing bro?"

It was Matt's older half-brother, Rick. Rick and Matt shared a father, Chris Chance, the CIA agent who had fallen in love with Matt's mother while on assignment in Bangkok though he had a wife and children back in Boston. Chris Chance had died in the Hezbollah terrorist bombing of the U.S. embassy in Beirut. Matt hadn't seen Rick since he first met him when he had made a visit to the states over a year before. Rick was on the operations side of the agency and, after Matt had a chance to brief him, had helped track down a rogue Bangkok station chief Matt had encountered on one of his cases.

They exchanged a handshake hug and then Rick sat down on the bench next to Matt.

"I'm doing great, except for jet lag and the fact that it's too hot and humid here. How do you folks stand it?"

"Actually 'we folks' find this to be a comfortable temperature. Can I ask what brings you to Thailand?"

Rick waved his hand at their park surroundings "You can ask, but right here and now it's not possible to answer. I'm here to invite you to meet with me and some of my colleagues tomorrow morning."

Matt was surprised. "Whoa, an invitation from your firm has some weight. Will this be a professional meeting? What's going on?"

"We'll have to hold that discussion until the meeting. Let's just say we have an interest in the case you were just involved in."

"That's got my attention. Where and when?"

"You'll be picked up at your apartment at 8 a.m. and, by the way, we understand there was another former army officer, a female chopper pilot, who was working with you. She's been invited to attend also, okay? Do you have a good opinion of her work?"

"Yeah, she's first class. Having her involved is fine with me. That case had a less than satisfactory ending. If there is hope of making it right, I'm sure we'll both be in."

CHAPTER FORTY-FOUR

The meeting was held at yet another safe house, though this time it was a Bangkok station safe house. Matt noted it was in a neighborhood of houses with high security block walls, entry gates and security cameras. The agency's security precautions wouldn't appear out of place here. As they drove through the gate Matt saw two black SUVs parked to the side of the house, one empty and one with two men seated in front. They didn't move as the SUV Matt had been picked up with parked at the front entrance of the large, flag stone exterior, house.

Rick opened the front door of the house when Matt's SUV drove up. He waved Matt into a large room off the entrance holding a round table with two people already sitting there. Jade was there and waved a hello to Matt.

"I see these guys captured you too. Do you think we can trust them?"

Matt laughed and pointed to Rick, "Well I think this one's okay. This is my brother Rick. We've worked together before."

Rick smiled at Jade. "As I told you, I promise, we're on the same team." He pointed to the other man at the table, who sat clicking the keys on a lap top computer. "This is Don. He has some special skills and heads the unit which is at the center of what we hope to do." Don, a slightly built man with thinning hair, a high forehead and horn rim glasses with thick lens, just looked up briefly and nodded to Matt and Jade. No smile, serious business.

Rick started the briefing.

"Due to your military service you both have had high U.S. government security clearances in the past. However, I'm obligated to advise you that the subject of this conversation and any remarks made here are covered under U.S. security regulations. There are strict laws and punishments governing the public disclosure of any of the material under discussion."

Matt and Jade glanced at each other with a we've both heard this before expression and nodded.

Rick continued. "Good. Now that that is out of the way let me brief you on the status of things, our plans and your potential role.

"I understand you have some of the background but let me start from the beginning. First the man you were hunting, his top aides and the two girls they kidnapped are no longer lodged in Thailand. They are now, to the best of our knowledge, in the Chinese Administrative Territory of Macau. The site where they are now houses the server and is the base for the cyber network used for trafficking and other international cybercrimes. As far as the Thai government is concerned they are now out of Thai reach. However, they are not out of the realm of Thai government interest. The station forwarded the background to Washington where it was decided that the activity in Macao is of operational interest to our government." Nodding towards Don, he said, "That is where we come in.

"Don is one of our best cyber warriors. He has a team with him and is backed, as necessary, by the full cyber security resources of the U.S. government. There will be a need for operatives on the ground in this program, so I'm here to oversee that. Don and I are partners, but it is his call as to what, if any, on the ground activity may be necessary in Macau to support him."

Matt, who felt a need to get involved in the conversation, said, "And?"

"And it was volunteered by the Thai authorities in our

handover discussions that, based on your recent involvement in this case and overall history, the two of you might be of use to the operation. I agreed, and you two did also, at least to the point of talking it over."

Rick continued. "It was decided since the rescue of the two girls and the apprehension of the monk had been part of the Thai government's information sharing deal, that a small team of operators would support the cyber team to see if extraction of the girls and the monk could be accomplished within the framework of attacking the dark web server site in Macau. However, the cyber team is running the operation. Nothing will be done which might interfere with their goal, which isn't to take down the site but rather to hijack it."

Here Chris turned to Don. "Can you summarize the target information for them."

Don nodded. "The target is one of the highest on the list, I would say up with the Russians, Chinese and Iranians. We are certain that the server is part of the North Korean cyber warfare agency known as Bureau 121, which comes under the Reconnaissance General Bureau of North Korea's military. I understand you have some background on their hacking history in order to raise funds. This activity is just a small part of their program which is primarily focused on South Korea, Japan and the U.S. The significance of this opening, no matter how small, is that through access to the computers at this site, we may gain access to their server and to deeper programs. The question is how to do it without alerting them or starting a cyber war, above the one that already exists, with the Chinese. Rick?"

Here he nodded to Rick. He had been allowed to assert his primacy and the importance of the operation. He was content to leave Rick to discuss any further information the two field agents, as he viewed them, needed to know.

Rick, a long-time veteran of the power games played within the agency, smiled and said, "Thank you."

Turning back to Jade and Matt he said. "Actually we have

some advantages if it's decided that we go in on the ground in Macao. Though it's administered by China the central government early on decided to leave it open to international activities, especially gambling. It is now the number one gambling site in the world. It is a uniquely active international playground. The Triads are allowed to continue activity as long as their gambling shake downs or loan sharking activities are done discretely. Many things are allowed or intentionally overlooked. An on the ground operation won't be easy but it does seem possible. You two bring certain skills to the game that we think make it easier for you to disappear into the international mix in Macao."

Now Jade decided to assert herself. She didn't know Rick and she had come away from her experiences in Iraq and Afghanistan with a somewhat wary view of agency operations. She decided to display her skepticism.

"My goodness, sir. What possible skills may I and this knuckle dragger bring to the table?"

Having started to become acclimated to Jade's edgy manner Matt just smiled. Rick, new to Jade's style, frowned and took it seriously.

"Uhh yes." He looked over at Don who was now on his phone. "Let's retire to the next room and discuss that."

CHAPTER FORTY-FIVE

As they walked into the adjoining room Matt looked at Jade and whispered, "Knuckle dragger? Really?"

She laughed. "Don't be upset, you're just a tool. I'm looking to get a rise out of the agency boys. Don't feel bad. I'm not done yet."

In the adjoining room they sat together on a sofa in front of a coffee table across from Rick who was sitting in an easy chair. The atmosphere immediately became less formal. Rick seemed to feel more comfortable away from Don. That helped Matt to relax a bit more but Jade was still on edge. She decided to continue on the attack. It wasn't her nature to be handled in any way. Before Rick could speak, she did.

"As I said, why the two of us?"

Rick, beginning to understand that attack was her nature, smiled.

"Good question. You're both familiar with some aspects of the operation, the monk and the girls he kidnapped as part of his dark web operation. The Thai DSI recommended you. I should say up front that in terms of skin tone you both fit into the Macao scene much better than any of our white corn-fed agency boys from Nebraska."

Jade laughed, "You mean what worked against us in the military may be of use now?"

Rick shrugged, looking to Matt for support.

"The simple answer is yes. Matt speaks Thai, looks somewhat Thai and, in this situation, can pass as one of many Thai gamblers who flock to Macau. You look Thai and Chinese enough to pass for either one and our background check shows you speak Cantonese from your home setting. That's the most common tongue in Macao though of course Pu Tong Hua or standard Chinese is now in vogue. In other words, you both can pass and disappear into the crowd in the gambling scene there. That is crucially important."

Matt spoke up, "My friend here has a point. Neither of us are spy material."

"No you aren't and we won't be asking you to spy or make contacts or recruit. That has, for the most part, been done through our Hong Kong operation. We have more details to work out but your presence will be sponsored by a rich Chinese attorney and gambler who has contacts and frequently fronts for the Shui Fong triad in Macau. We have had occasion to work with him before and he has been reliable. He will handle the gambling and triad scene. You two will be partners who like the gambling scene but are just there as guests of the Chinese attorney. In other words, you will be a couple."

Jade, looking over to Matt said, "In other words, I'm to be his chick."

Rick laughed "At least in public, to carry out the legend. Can you do that?"

"Yeah I guess so but let's get one thing straight. I don't wear dresses."

Rick raised his eyebrows a bit but quickly went along. "Okay, no dresses, just dress to fit into the gambling scene. These are all basically night clubs."

Matt asked, "More seriously, in what scenario do you see us being involved?"

"There are aspects of the operation that are still being developed, but we believe that through the Shui Fong triad we have found where the kidnapped girls are being held. We believe that site to be the focus of the kidnapping scheme you worked as well as the group that oversees gambling and moneylending here in Thailand. I understand you have also had direct contact with the local gambling and loan sharking connections here in Thailand. You'll be with the team that goes into the site and rescues the girls. At present that is the sum of what you need to know. If you are on the team, we will have more details when we meet with the operational contact in Hong Kong. Now, I want you to take a night to think it over. Tomorrow you can let me know if you are in or not. If you are, be ready to move quickly."

Matt and Jade looked at each other nodding simultaneously and speaking together. "I'm in."

Rick laughed, nodded, and looking at Matt, said, "That's good to know but you can tell me that again after you've had a night to think it over. There is significant danger here. The triads, especially at one of their bases, are not to be messed with. They have taken a much quieter surface tone in Macau after the Chinese takeover but their ability to bring violence, when they choose to, is still there. "

CHAPTER FORTY-SIX

Rick walked out with them and put them in one of the black SUVs telling the driver, "Take them wherever they want to go." Nodding to Matt and Jade he said, "I'll be in contact in the morning." Then he walked away.

Jade asked Matt, "What do you think? Where can we go to talk?"

Matt nodded towards the driver letting her know he wanted to hold off on the talk for now. He then directed the driver to take them to the Terminal 21 building on Sukhumvit avenue at the very busy Asoke intersection. It wasn't their destination, but close enough. Any conversation could be held until then, out of the driver's hearing.

The street near the shopping high rise and the train station were, as always, hot, dirty and noisy. After the SUV dropped them off Matt turned to Jade, "Exactly my thought, we need to talk. There was more to that meeting than met the eye. Let's go to Hustlers. It's early and it'll be quiet."

"Good. I want you to catch up with Apple now. She trusts you and wanted to see you again. She should be in to work soon."

They started the walk up to the BTS station, made their way through the throng of commuters lining up at the entry gates, and over and across the street to the entry of the Times Square building. Hustlers was down the steps to the basement.

Inside, relaxing in the cool air of Hustlers, virtually empty now at midday, they ordered some coffee and sat down.

Matt watched the day waitress walk away and then turned to Jade.

"Sorry for appearing to be paranoid but in dealing with the agency it never hurts to be paranoid."

"Even with your brother involved?"

"I wouldn't be involved if my brother wasn't part of their team here. That is just the point. Rick was giving us clear signals this morning that indicated this operation is not as simple as the line he officially shared with us."

"Like what?"

"Like telling us openly that he is not in charge of the operation, that the cyber boss is. Which makes sense. The U.S. government would not be involved here just to rescue two kidnapped Thai girls or to arrest a criminal Thai monk. I don't think they or the Thai government really give a damn about the girls. I suppose the Thai government would be happy to see the monk brought down but again, the cyber part of the operation is driving all of this."

"And?"

"And, I think what Rick was warning us about was that if we go, we're only a peripheral part of the operation as the two governments see it. We'd like to complete our original mission, get the girls out, put the monk out of commission and help to shut down the gambling and loan shark network at its source. My feeling is we may be used that way or we may not, but we're signing up to be used no matter what. We're cover for the real program. Rick was doing his job to recruit us but, when he told us to take a night to think it over, he was warning us at the same time."

Jade was quiet for a moment, looking out the front window of Hustlers at the street activity. Finally, she turned back to Matt and asked, "You trust Rick?"

"Completely, but he warned us he's not in overall charge."

"So, it won't be the first time to be used, will it? Let's see if we can get the girls out and put down the monk however we can."

"Okay we're in. Good, while we're waiting for Apple let's see if I can show you how to shoot some pool. It's easy to learn a little bit about it, but maddening to try and learn a lot."

CHAPTER FORTY-SEVEN

Arriving in Hong Kong harbor at night is akin to attending a fantasy light show. The multi-colored lights of the skyscrapers and the neon advertising signs on the main island compete with the ad beacons from the Kowloon side of the harbor, both blinking a video scream for the traveler's attention. The cumbersome, green, ferry boats, plying their way between Hong Kong island and the Kowloon terminal, lead the water borne parade of smaller vessels bobbing in all directions around large cargo ships moored in the harbor.

Rick was leading the way. He had supplied the air tickets for Matt and Jade. He also told them to use their regular passports for entry to Hong Kong. New ID and whatever else they needed for Macau would be provided in Hong Kong. They had taken the train from the airport to the Kowloon stop where they waded through the massed, seemingly pulsating, crowd to the exit up to the street. Rick was taking them by foot to a safe house in the Kowloon area. A meeting had been arranged with one of the agency staff based in Hong Kong.

As they walked, carrying the light handbags, enough for the three days Rick had told them to prepare for, Jade sniffed the air enjoying the salty tang of the ocean water. She had told Matt she had no love for the water, she wasn't a good swimmer, but she liked the proximity to it, viewed from a safe distance.

There was no talking. Rick focused on his path and keeping

173

track of any possible surveillance. He walked them into several hotels and out the side exits, then back up the hill towards Nathan Road. After a hundred meters, going up Nathan Road in Tsim Sha Tsui and refusing two offers of counterfeit Rolex watches by eager street peddlers, he brought them to a narrow side street and turned into it.

Halfway down the street Rick turned into a doorway with a red light outside which led up a narrow flight of stairs to a second-floor landing with dim lighting. There he knocked on a door. After a minute a young Chinese man opened the door, nodded to Rick and motioned them into the room. Once inside the man signaled them to stay put and disappeared into a back room.

A second later, a plump, fortyish Chinese man strode into the room. He greeted Rick with a big smile. "Hey man, we don't see you here for long time. We finally have something that interest you hey?"

"Yeah Ben, something of interest for sure." He then turned to Matt and Jade, "This is Ben, he is the man making arrangements for your visit to Macau. Ben do you have the entry papers for these two?"

"Yes, we are ready, also transportation is arranged for tomorrow to the Venetian in Macau and I'll be accompanying them to make the introduction to our attorney friend Mr. Choi."

"Wonderful. Let's all sit down. Ben, can you listen in while I brief them and correct anything I get wrong?"

Ben nodded and pointed the group to a round table and chairs at the back of the room. Just then there was another knock on the door. The younger Chinese man came out of the back room and opened the door to another Chinese man but one older, in his forties, skinny and shorter. It was the first street side vendor who had offered to sell Rick a watch. The man came in, just nodded to Ben and, along with the other man, walked into the back room.

Ben smiled at Rick. "That was Mr. Li. He covered your walk and says you are clear."

Rick looked to Matt and Jade "You see, we're in good hands. Now let me fill you in. Ben will be taking you to a casino in Macau tomorrow to introduce you to the man I told you about, a lawyer, who works with the Shui Fong triad group. There are several significant triads in Macau, the Shui Fong and the 14K are the two biggest. The two groups have fought over the years for influence and access to the casinos. In the old days they would go around shooting each other on the streets but, when the mainland Chinese took over Macau from the Portuguese in 1999, they forced these two gangs into a truce. While they still compete, it is done in a somewhat more normal, commercial manner. However, the 14K has recently made online forays into the dark web and into bitcoin manipulation, stepping to some extent on the toes of the Shui Fong's own bitcoin operation. The Shui Fong want to send a message to the 14K. Ben's sources within Shui Fong have information that the monk, his aides and the two kidnapped women he brought with him are being held in a mansion and computer site operated by the 14K triad. The mansion is owned by a somewhat famous gang leader, Won, Kuok-Koi, also known as Broken-Tooth Won from a car accident when he lost control of the car during a gang shooting on the highway.

"Ben has been kept aware as the Shui Fong developed their plans for a raid on the 14K mansion and cyber site. This is the server used by the North Koreans in their cyber-attacks and is linked to the dark web posts in Thailand. Your rescue mission will be cover for the cyber raid on the site. I can't go into details on the other aspects of the raid."

Matt spoke up. "What about the monk? Is he part of our responsibility or will others handle him?"

Rick smiled, "That's a good way to put it. Others will handle him. Don't worry about that. You will be briefed further on the raid details in Macau. Our cyber group will have two guys going in with you and the Shui Feng group. You will coordinate with the cyber guys and get whatever weapons you need in Macau."

Jade asked, "Whoa, wait, what about extraction? Once it's over, I presume the Shui Fong boys go home. How do Matt and I and the girls get out afterwards?"

"That will be briefed in Macau but I will be on hand for the extraction. It will be done smoothly and quickly from the raid site, okay? We'll have eyes on you."

Rick addressed Ben. "Is that all correct Ben?"

Ben smiled at Rick. "Very thoroughly as always Mr. Rick. You leave now. I make sure these two are prepared and get to the meeting place at the Venetian tomorrow."

Rick nodded, "Thanks Ben." He continued, looking at Matt and Jade. "You're in good hands. Ben has saved me in the past and he'll make sure you are okay tomorrow. Get some sleep here. It used to be a brothel. They have plenty of extra rooms. I have to go to another meeting. I'll be around and in touch if need be."

Matt looked over to Jade, thinking I shouldn't do this, a small smile playing around his lips as he remembered the cover story that they were a couple. "Well dear, which side of the bed do you prefer?"

Jade snorted in amusement, "Not gonna happen ranger boy. Maybe you can find one of the former occupants to help you with your personal problems. I don't imagine it will take long."

Ben had seen too much of Americans wise cracking to each other over the years to be surprised or concerned over the exchange. "Don't worry. You'll each have your own comfortable room and bath. Very nice. Important thing is to be well rested tomorrow morning. The next few days will be very busy."

CHAPTER FORTY-EIGHT

Leung Somboon was very dissatisfied. He was not being treated with the respect he deserved. Though the triad mansion in Macao was certainly the haven he had sought, he was being treated as just another guest. He was used to respect which bordered on, indeed often was, devotion. This was not the case with these Chinese gangsters.

Managing the dark web site in Thailand had been the responsibility of one of his devoted followers. While Leung Somboon had known that the final destination for the girls his followers brought in was brokered through a Chinese gang in Macau, he certainly had not been involved in any direct contact with them. The negotiations with the Chinese and the management issues had all been handled by key followers.

He now found the Chinese arrogant. They had bragged to him and made it clear that their site was the nexus of many dark web schemes. The operation to bring young girls from Thailand was just a small, though enjoyable, diversion. They treated him as if he was a pimp not the head of a major religious sect.

He had decided to confront Mr. Won and asked for a private meeting.

One of the gun-carrying men that had been present at his arrival escorted him to an office on the second floor of the mansion.

Mr. Won, smoking a cigarette, looked up from his desk and blew out a puff of smoke as Leung Somboon was shown in.

"Ahhh, my guest. What can I do for you? I hope all the arrangements are comfortable."

Leung Somboon turned away from the smoke, thinking 'Chinese barbarians', but tried hard not to show his discomfort. "The arrangements are comfortable, thank you, but I have to say I'm uncomfortable being away from my work and unable to communicate with my many followers. It's time for me and my staff to move on. We'll leave the two young women as your guests. I'm sure they can be of use here."

"Well of course Leung Somboon. We will make arrangements, but it may be quite expensive. What is your idea?"

"I understand there is an airport here in Macau which can accommodate planes large enough to fly to Europe. I have followers and a temple in the South of France. I would ask that arrangements be made to charter a plane for my staff and me to leave some night when the airport is at its quietest. You understand cost is not an issue."

"Ahh, yes. We can make such arrangements including bypassing security and customs."

"How soon can we go?"

"Please give us a few days. The plane is easily arranged. Private travel to and from Macau sometimes seems to exceed public travel. The security arrangements need to be seen to however."

"As soon as possible. I'm eager to get on with my work."

Mr. Won smiled, "As you ask. Just a few days for arrangements okay?"

Leung Somboon nodded and left, going to speak with his staff who were waiting in a private area of the mansion that had been turned over to them.

The staff he had brought along to Macau turned to him as he walked back into the room.

"I have spoken with Mr. Won. We will be leaving soon. We will be going to France to work from the temple there. Let my followers there know we will be coming."

The senior aide asked, "When shall we expect to arrive?"

"I'm not sure. Mr. Won could not give me a fixed date, he just asked for some time to prepare. I don't trust him. He is up to too many things. Doing business at arms-length was acceptable. Being here, under his control is not. However, we have no choice but to wait for now."

At his desk Mr. Won was watching and listening through the camera system installed throughout the mansion. He thought to himself, *How stupid this religious imposter is. Before he goes anywhere we will find out his market value and see what deal can be made for him.*

Leung Somboon would be leaving soon, but only when it would be profitable for Broken-Tooth Won.

CHAPTER FORTY-NINE

Matt could feel that Jade was tense as they approached the Venetian hotel. He felt the same, thinking yeah, this is game on now. When they entered the lobby though, that was forgotten, as Jade stood awe struck and looked around the Venetian lobby.

"Wow. We should be paying your brother's firm for the vacation here. This must be the gambling Mecca of the world."

Jade continued circling in place, taking in the high vaulted ceiling with its ornate main fresco surrounded by a circle of equally impressive smaller frescoes. The very bright lighting and the gold paint on the remaining ceiling spaces, the walls and stairs were designed to impress and overwhelm all who came in and they succeeded. The golden globe and Hercules statue in the lobby center provided photo bait for a stream of mostly Chinese visitors.

Matt agreed. "Yeah, spectacular. It's very Chinese, gold, gold and more gold. This is the first time I've been to Macau in years, but of all the new buildings this has to be on the top of the list in terms of its Vegas showmanship. It's now the largest hotel and casino site in Macau. I doubt we'll have much of a vacation though."

They had made an attempt to dress for the part within the limits of their respective personal identities. Jade was wearing a black pant suit and a long-sleeved white cotton blouse buttoned up to the neck. Her hair was straight back in a ponytail. She wore no makeup and her jewelry consisted of a small diamond in her left year. As far as she was concerned she had stretched the 'chick' persona to its limit. Matt noted the suit jacket was a bit loose, leaving enough room for a holster when the time came.

Matt had gone military smart casual. He was wearing gray dress pants, and a dark blue blazer over a light blue shirt open at the collar. There was no way he could bring himself to wear a tie.

They were both also wearing miniature GPS tracker chips so their whereabouts could be tracked by Rick and his team. Jade's was in a medal disc that connected her bra in front. Matt's was in a button on the back of the slacks he was wearing. These chips were in addition to their cell phones which were their first line of security.

Ben, who had gone to the high roller check in desk to see to the room arrangements, came hustling over. "It has been arranged as our friend promised. We'll go up to your suite and we'll be joined there but we need to wait here a minute. I have some men sweeping the suite."

After a few minutes two men in black suits and carrying brief cases came out of the elevator bank and walked towards the lobby entrance. Neither of them looked at Ben and his two charges. One paused to adjust his tie for a second and then continued out.

"Okay we're clear. Let's go. Remember you're a Thai couple. Speak only Thai and English from here on." He turned to Jade, "It's best if they don't know that you understand Cantonese."

On the way over to Macau, with the car crossing the newly built bridge, Ben had given them their ID for the operation in Macau. They were now carrying Thai passports, appropriately stamped, and some backup driving and credit documents. The lawyer working with the Shui Fong triad would be the only one who knew their rescue mission. Other triad members they met would understand they were here representing triad related gambling interests in Thailand. Many, if not most of the overseas visitors coming to the gaming tables in Macau had connections to illegal gambling at their home bases.

Any others in Macau would be given to understand that they were a Thai couple, who had come to Macau for a pleasure trip and some gambling.

CHAPTER FIFTY

When Ben opened the doors they found the suite was, as was everything at the Venetian, opulent, both in size for the two separate bedrooms and the quality of the furnishings. Jade stopped in the lounge area of the suite asking, "Do we really have to leave here? Can't we just do all our business on site?"

Matt was getting used to her ways and just replied, "No dear. There is business to see to."

"Very funny. You drop the dear approach and I'll drop the knuckle dragger line."

"Deal."

"Ben, what's the next step?"

"Put away your gear. We have two other team members who will join us here. Then we'll go to meet the lawyer, Mr. Choi. He'll discuss the next step the triad guys want to take. I expect they'll be moving soon. Maybe even tonight."

Matt saw a briefcase standing on the coffee table. It was there when they came in the room. Suspicious package? Ben saw Matt looking and walked over to it and opened it up.

"My colleagues left this for us. Matt, Rick said you prefer the HK pistols. One gun is an HK P 30 for you. Jade you get your preferred army standard Beretta. Four magazines each and shoulder holsters are included."

Matt said, "I feel better." Jade smiled and nodded her head. "Dam right."

A few minutes later there was a knock on the door. Ben answered the door and welcomed in two Caucasian men. Both men were over six feet tall. One, slightly taller than the other, was wearing glasses. They were dressed simply in blue polo shirts and khaki slacks. No greeting. They just nodded to Ben.

As the men entered Ben turned to Matt and Jade and said, "These are the technicians who will go along with the raid. Pointing to the taller man, he said, "His name is Tom. His partner is Jerry."

When Jade laughed at the obvious false names, Ben smiled and gestured to Matt. "You understand this is somebody's sense of humor. But the point is made, they don't need to know your names and you don't need to know theirs."

Then he turned back to include the two men also. "The important point is that when the time comes, it may be very fast moving and confusing. Now you know who is on your side and who you must help if need be."

Matt asked, "Who will be taking us in?"

"A key point thank you. You two," nodding to Matt and Jade, "will be meeting soon with the lawyer. He will have two experienced men from the triad with him. Their job will be to get you in, and get you out when the time is right. They'll know nothing of your respective missions except that it is important to the triad."

Ben looked at the group. Nods all around. Then he focused on Matt and Jade.

"This is important. You have a mission you want to complete, however their mission," pointing to Ben and Jerry, "is the primary reason for our being here. If there is doubt, you drop what you are doing and make sure they get in and out successfully."

Matt and Jade looked at each other. As they expected they were being used but they knew that coming in. They both shook their heads yes.

Ben said "Good." He waved the two men to the door. "Go stand by in your rooms. You will be called when it's time to leave. Have your bags packed."

Rick was nearby, also in Macau, with a small team staying in a hotel not so elaborate or expensive as the Venetian. He was following Matt and Jade with the GPS locator. He had plans for their extraction but it depended on knowing their location so he could guide them out. Now his team was waiting. It was up to the Shui Fong triad to decide when to move. They had already declared to Ben that the mansion would be empty when they raided it. That the monk and two girls were being held there was just good fortune. Rick hoped they could achieve what Matt and Jade wanted, the rescue of the girls, but that was just a side show to provide cover. The important goal was to get his tech team inside with time to install some software.

The issue was the timing. They needed the 14K leader to be out of the mansion when they raided. The goal for the Shui Fong was to send a message to Broken-Tooth Won, not to declare outright war. They also did not want to attract the attention of the Chinese military administering Macau.

CHAPTER FIFTY-ONE

Rising from a sofa in his suite to greet them, lawyer Choi was a well-tailored picture of the rewards of gambling wealth. He was slim and in his late fifties. In addition to his expensive grey pin-striped suit he wore gold rings on both hands. The ring on his right hand had a large emerald stone implanted in it. On his bespoke suit the left sleeve was pulled up a bit to ensure the gold Rolex he wore would be visible. His black hair was slicked back, which, along with the excessive epicanthal fold of his eyelids, gave him a snake-like appearance.

As Matt and Jade walked into his suite behind Ben, he gave them a smile, which was only on his lips. The rest of this face was rigid. He exuded an aurora of danger, which both Matt and Jade felt immediately.

He spoke in English, "So you are the Thai couple Ben mentioned. How do you like the Venetian?"

Matt answered for the Thai couple. "Impressive. I'm sure there is much we could enjoy here, regrettably we're here on business."

"So I understand. So let's get straight to that." Turning he called to the next room and two Chinese men entered. They were lean, one of medium height, the other about six foot tall. Both were wearing black slacks with white short sleeved shirts worn loosely outside their trousers. They came in and nodded to Choi. Their arms were covered in tattoos. The tall one had a long scar on his left cheek. The lawyer spoke to them in Cantonese waving one arm towards Matt, Jade and Ben while he spoke. Then he turned back to his visitors.

"These two men are brothers and dependable business associates of mine. They do not speak English, only Cantonese, but when the time comes you just go with them. They and their men will take you to the scene and control the activity. Just follow them in and do your business. We expect little trouble as there will only be a few of Broken-Tooth's men on site, but, you never know, do you?" With the last statement his mouth smiled, but again, not the eyes.

The two men said nothing, they just stared at Matt and Jade, especially Jade. Jade was uncomfortable with their stare and turned away from the men, closer to Matt.

Ben answered, "Good. Mr. Choi, you are efficient as always. Just let us know when it's time. My visitors will be standing by in their room."

"We expect to go in a matter of hours. The brothers are just waiting for a final report on the status of the house. Once we are sure that Broken-Tooth Won is not on the scene they will move." Looking at Matt and Jade he said, "Be ready to go quickly."

Back in their room Jade quickly turned and confronted Matt and Ben. "I don't like this. I don't like the way these guys looked or looked at me. Something's wrong here."

Matt shrugged and answered, "Because they were staring at you? The reality is they're bad guys, you're a new woman on their turf, and will be packing a gun on the raid. They should stare."

"Yeah, well it's more than that. It was creepy. Scar Face was looking at me as if I was one of their girls. It's not a comfortable feeling."

Ben, who had been watching them talk, stepped in, "They will be focused on their job. I wouldn't worry about anything else. They are there to neutralize Broken-Tooth's staff and help you to get the girls out. Once they see you with a gun in your hand that will put you in a different category in their mind. Don't worry."

Jade didn't fully accept that. "Yeah, he's Scar Face to me and I'll keep an eye on him all the way. You have to work with people like this. I don't."

Turning to include Matt, Ben continued, "When the time comes I will take care of your bags and check out of the room. You will not be coming back here."

Jade asked, "Where will we be going? Remember we will be herding the two girls and possibly the monk along."

"Mr. Rick will be following you electronically and will be nearby. He'll call on your burner phone when the time comes to leave the site. The Shui Fong guys will go their own way. They have studied the interior map of the building. It should go down fast. The main thing is to get away from the mansion before any 14K have time to react. All of it must be done very quickly."

CHAPTER FIFTY-TWO

The knock on the door came soon after. They had only a few hours of rest when, at midnight, the scar-faced one of the two brothers appeared at the door and spoke with Ben who turned to them.

"It's time to go. Follow this man. He will take you to your ride. Good luck."

Jade asked him, "Will we see you again?"

"It's not in the plan. Mr. Rick will handle things now."

They went out into the hall and to a freight elevator where Scar Face's brother was waiting to take them all down. He led them out a back entrance of the hotel to a large black Mercedes Benz sedan which was waiting there behind another black Mercedes. One of the brothers got into the first car and it moved off. They got in the back of the second car and Scar Face got in front and spoke to the driver.

Jade understood him. As they moved off she leaned over to Matt and whispered to him in English, "This is it. He said to go straight to the target." Scar Face turned around and looked at her and shook his head. Clearly no talking was allowed.

They quickly left the glare of the Venetian and the other nearby casinos behind and soon were on narrow back roads heading south. This was through an area known as Colane Village on a road that led to oceanfront homes, parks and beaches.

Matt, who had studied the maps prior to their departure, leaned over and whispered this to Jade. Again Scar Face turned and shook his head, this time glaring at them and swearing in Cantonese. Jade decided not to translate for Matt.

They came to an area of darkness and Matt guessed it was one of the parks near the beach areas. On the way to the park they had passed several mansions overlooking the ocean scattered along the road. They swerved around a gate into the park and found the first car stopped alongside the road a bit further inside the park. Four men from the first car were already out of the car and waiting for them. Two of them were the technicians, Tom and Jerry.

Scar Face, leading Matt and Jade, got out as well as the driver and indicated they should follow him. The four Shui Fong men were dressed completely in black. Each had a red handkerchief tied around his neck and at a word from the leader they brought them up to mask their faces. Two of them were carrying Heckler and Koch automatic rifles. Matt's immediate thought was, these guys aren't playing games. The other triad men, Scar Face and his brother, were carrying handguns with silencers. Matt and Jade drew their own weapons. Tom and Jerry were unarmed. Gun play wasn't their thing.

Scar Face motioned his men towards a narrow dirt track that led to a break in the park fence. It was show time.

Matt glanced over to Jade to encourage her. "Stay close, okay?"

Jade gave him a raised eyebrow look as if to say 'of course dummy' but just answered, "Sounds good to me."

They walked through a wooded section and came to the park boundary. The mansion was only fifty yards from the fence line across a well-manicured lawn with no bushes in sight. Scar Face stopped the group and studied the mansion and then moved through a hole in the fence signaling them to follow. There were a couple of faint lights within the building and security lights on the back and front, but not on the side to which they quickly moved. A thin blanket of cloud covered the half moon. Matt had been worried about dogs raising an alarm, but there no dogs, no sounds. As they closed on the building Matt wondered how they would get in without raising an alarm, but the answer came quickly. One of the Shui Fong men just reached out and opened the door. It was unlocked. An inside job.

Inside there was a corridor with dimmed ceiling lights and a T junction at the end. Tom and Jerry followed their two men down to the end and went left. Scar Face and his brother went to the end of the corridor and turned to the right with Matt and Jade following closely. At the end of the corridor there were two doors, one on the right and one on the left. Scar Face paused and indicated to Matt and Jade that they should go in the door on the left but held up his hand for them to pause a second while he put his hand on the doorknob on the right-side door. Then he nodded to Matt and Jade to go ahead on their side while he pushed open the door in front of him.

Matt moved quickly to open the door and found a bedroom. There was a night light on. The two Thai girls who had been kidnapped were laying on a bed asleep. One jumped up as Matt and Jade came in. Matt spoke to her in Thai. "Don't be afraid. We're here to take you home. Wake up your friend and get your clothes on. We have to move now."

Behind him, in the room across the corridor, Matt heard the repeated puff, puff, puff, of the silenced pistols. Killing, unless necessary, hadn't been part of the plan. Matt turned towards the door behind him. He could see, through the open door opposite, several bodies lying on the floor, but he could make out no weapons. Then Scar Face and his brother appeared coming from out of the room. They brought no one with them.

Jade had moved forward and had put her pistol away while she was helping the girls to get ready to move. As Matt turned back to encourage the girls to move faster, a white flash went off in his head and then all stopped.

CHAPTER FIFTY-THREE

Jade was helping the girls get dressed to go when she heard the thunk of one of the Shui Fong guys sapping Matt on the head and then Matt's gun and body hitting the ground almost immediately. She turned around putting a hand on the Beretta and started to pull it out. Both of the brothers were standing with their guns pointed at her. There was no play. She took her hand off the Beretta. Scar Face smiled and nodded. Obedience was what he wanted.

He didn't know that Jade understood Cantonese but it was the only language he knew besides the gun. He shouted at Jade to bring the two girls and they were leaving now.

Jade was sick, she'd come to rescue the girls. Now she was being forced to help deliver them to a new gang to exploit them. There was no choice. Don't panic. She turned back to the girls and told them "Don't be afraid. I'll take care of you." The girls were in shock and didn't believe her or their new situation. They had to move. Jade grabbed them both by an arm and started to walk them out. As she passed by Scar Face's brother he reached over, pulled her Beretta out of its holster and dropped it on the floor. He followed behind and pushed the girls along as Scar Face rushed down the hallway. At the T junction the two other gang members were coming back out and joined them. Jade and the two girls were hustled out the door to the fence opening into the park and along the dirt trail they had come in on. The two cars were waiting. Jade and the two girls were pushed into the back of the second and the cars sped out of the park. The whole action from entry to departure had taken less than ten minutes.

Jade was in shock but clung to the positive thought that, for whatever reason, they hadn't killed Matt. He would be coming after them, she knew that.

CHAPTER FIFTY-FOUR

Matt twisted on the floor, his head hurt and his face was wet from someone throwing cold water on his head.

"Hey bro. It's time to wake up. We've got to get out of here before the other bad guys come or we'll both be in trouble." It was Rick pulling on Matt's shirt to get him upright.

Matt was trying to respond but was still dazed. "What happened? What's going on?"

"No time to explain buddy but our bad guys turned out to be somewhat undependable." Rick extended Matt's Sig Sauer to him, "Here take this, at least they didn't take your gun. You were lying on top of it."

Rick turned to another man standing in the door holding an automatic weapon. "Get a hand under him and let's move him outside."

Matt was coming around, but they still needed to propel him along, through the door he had entered and back out towards the park. Inside the park, where the two Shui Fong cars had been stopped, there was a black SUV with two Chinese men standing by. Rick helped Matt into the back seat, while telling the others, "Move, move, move." They jumped in and the SUV roared off. Matt slumped back again, only semi-conscious.

Matt wasn't aware of time, it could have been five minutes later or fifty minutes, he didn't know. He was dizzy. He held tightly to the seat to keep his balance. They pulled through some iron gates into a courtyard. Again Rick and the other man half lifted him and half propelled him up some steps and through the doors of a large stone fronted house. There were no lights on outside. They led him into a brightly-lit room and sat him down on a sofa. Matt, slowly regaining consciousness, fought to stay upright.

He looked towards Rick standing over him. "What happened?"

"Actually that's what we want to ask you first. Can you give me the story?"

Matt nodded and his head hurt so he stopped. He ran through the story to the point where the lights went out on him. Then looked back to Rick for an explanation.

While he was talking a medic came into the room and started examining the bloody patch on the back of his head. Matt stayed still so the medic could work but otherwise ignored him.

"So what happened?"

"Uhhh, we're still trying to get a full grip on that. Basically it seems as if our bad guys saw the three women as an opportunity and decided they could do their own business. The guys working for the monk weren't so attractive I guess. They were all put down. I believe they left you behind so that, as a Thai come to rescue the girls, you would take the blame when the 14K guys returned. When we got there we couldn't find any sign of the monk but, with his guys all dead, I would think he's not in a good position with the 14K."

"What three women? Jade and I only found two in the room."

"Well that's the really bad news. We suspect they view Jade as the third woman, to be disposed of as the other two. She wasn't in the house when we got there and her gun was left on the floor." Here Rick lifted his shirt and displayed Jade's Berretta tucked in his waistband.

"What about the other two guys?"

"You mean Tom and Jerry?"

Matt nodded and then winced at the pain.

"They were completely unaware of what was going on with you and Jade. Their guards just left them after showing them into the computer center. There was nobody attending to the equipment which we find somewhat suspicious but it made our access much easier. Thankfully the two gang guys didn't bother with Tom and Jerry. They were left to finish their business. After a few minutes, they found their way out to the deserted park and reported in just as we were coming to find out what happened to you. They heard nothing and saw nothing."

"How did you know something had happened to me?"

"Your GPS track stayed in the same place while Jade's moved out of the building and out of the area."

"Where is she. We have to go get her."

Here Rick looked at the medic who had cleaned the cut on Matt's head and was putting some coagulant gel on it. The medic looked at Rick and shrugged his shoulders, giving it the classic 'On you guys, not on me.'

"We're moving some resources into the area where we have her last GPS signal. We don't want obvious movement around the scene to alert the gang members, but our guys will be in position before we get there."

"Let's get going."

"You sure you can handle it? This will be hard and fast."

Matt started to shake his head yes and then winced and stopped. "I'm fine. Let's get on with this. We have no idea what these guys may be doing."

"Let's go."

CHAPTER FIFTY-FIVE

Jade and the two girls were not the only ones being held captive. On the northern side of the Macau Administrative Zone, Luang Somboon was being given the experience he and his followers had given so many young Thai girls. He was being sold.

Broken Tooth Won had invited the monk to accompany him to a meeting with the key person responsible for arranging the clearances for his night flight out of Macau. The invitation was of the sort that could not be refused. Leung Somboon was offended at the tone of the invitation but, in any case, was eager to join his supporters at the temple in France. If this was a necessary step he would go along. Luang Somboon's key aide had also come along to accompany his boss and to handle the details of the arrangements, such as payment.

They were led through a security gate in a cinder block walled compound, into a modestly-sized brick house which had two Chinese army soldiers standing guard on either side of the front door. Broken Tooth Won spoke to them and they opened the door and one of the soldiers entered before them and walked past an entryway sitting room and down a corridor to a double-doored room. He knocked on the door, opened it slightly and spoke to the occupant, then he turned and nodded to Broken Tooth Won. As they walked into the room Leung Somboon could see that it was essentially an office. Behind a large desk sitting in the back center of the room, sat a man in the uniform of a Chinese army officer. A People's Republic of China flag was on a short staff in the corner of the room. Leung Somboon could not know it but this man was one of the senior officers administrating affairs in Macau. He was responsible for seeing that all matters in the Macau gambling world were conducted in a manner acceptable to the Chinese overseers along with appropriate payments for the protection received. Maintaining contact with the triad heads was included in his responsibilities and had led to this profit opportunity.

Another man, in a black, well-tailored civilian suit, sat at a chair and table on the side of the room smoking a cigarette. The man represented the Macau business interests of the Thai generals Leung Somboon hated so much. His primary work was to keep track of a prominent exiled Thai politician and his supporters when they met in Macau. Tonight he was there to witness the completion of the transaction for Leung Somboon. It was a deal for which the Thai government intelligence service had paid over five million dollars to the parties involved.

A few seconds after they walked into the room the two soldiers who had been standing guard came into the room, closed the doors behind them and stood with their backs to the door. Leung Somboon didn't pay attention to them, he was waiting to be properly greeted by the officer behind the desk. However, except for a quick glance, the officer ignored him.

Speaking to the man sitting on the side, the officer asked in standard Chinese, "Is this the man who needs to be re-educated?"

The man merely nodded yes.

The officer turned back to Broken Tooth Won. "Satisfactory. You have completed your end of the transaction. My men will take it from here."

Broken Tooth Won nodded and turned, walking towards the door, as the two soldiers came up and took Leung Somboon and his aide by their arms. Broken Tooth Won opened the door and walked out without further word to Leung Somboon.

The monk understood that something had gone very wrong

but he didn't understand the Chinese dialect spoken and had no idea that he was going to disappear into the Chinese gulag system. The military junta in Thailand had purchased him and, by entrusting the Chinese to keep him out of sight, had just disposed of one threat to their grip on power. In the slang of the Bangkok police state, he had been 'disappeared.'

CHAPTER FIFTY-SIX

As they drove along the dimly lit, virtually empty streets, Rick spoke on the phone to his team members and then to Matt.

"The location we're headed to is an isolated private property located on the ocean a few miles further down the coast. My team is monitoring the road in both directions but staying out of sight. There is a boat ramp and access from the ocean which we have eyes on but it's presently dark and there are no signs of activity. There are lights on inside the building and two cars parked in the front area. Except for the GPS tracker showing that Jade is in the building we have no idea how many people are inside."

Matt was becoming more alert and aware of the situation. Also he was becoming angry with himself. How could he have allowed himself to be ambushed? He had told Jade to stay close and then failed to do the job of protecting her and the girls. He wanted vengeance. He wanted to finish the job.

"What is the plan? Do you have enough men to assault the building?"

Rick smiled, his younger brother was always the aggressive one. "Well the new plan is to improvise, which we're doing starting now. We had originally planned for a water borne extraction but had positioned it for the mansion you went into before. We are now in the process of moving those assets into position on the ocean near the mansion Jade is in. That is taking a few minutes but they should be in place by the time we get there. Enough men? Well we'll find that out soon. We'll certainly have enough firepower."

"How soon will we be on the scene?"

"We are only ten minutes away. At least Jade's GPS tracking device is only ten minutes away. If they found that and removed it, we don't know where they might have gone."

"Well they're not going to get that device off easily. You know it's attached to her bra. The guy who wants to remove it will have a fight on his hands he won't believe."

Chapter Fifty-Seven

Jade was still wearing her bra with the GPS device attached but otherwise the situation didn't look promising. She didn't know which was the worst problem, the guards or the girls.

Two of the triad members had come into their room with them. It was Scar Face and his brother who had taken them to an upstairs bedroom in the mansion. The other two men on the team had been told to wait downstairs with the two gang members who had been on site, and to break open the whiskey. It was a time for celebration. They could relax with the girls and turn them over to the gang boss later. The boss would decide their eventual use, possibly there would be enough money paid to ransom them. It didn't matter. Women were a saleable commodity, especially young and beautiful women. He and his men had done their job, it was time to relax and enjoy.

The two brothers had put their guns on a chair near the door to the room. Now they stood appraising Jade and the girls. They both expected the two young girls would be compliant and not difficult to handle. However, Jade looked as if she would be a problem. Scar Face liked that thought. It would be good to tame a wild horse. He was confident of his ability and he became more aroused. This was an experience he had enjoyed many times before.

Jade was still trying to calm the girls. They were semi-hysterical. Stupidly, at least to Jade's mind, they had immediately gone over and sat on the big bed in the room. Jade had yelled at them to stand up and get away from the bed, but they had just looked at her vacantly, not understanding her point. They had been captive long enough that compliance was all they understood.

The girls, holding hands now, stared at the two guards. Their eyes were bright with fear, but they just sat still.

Jade thought to herself, they're frozen, like deer in the headlights. They'll be no help. I have to do something or it's going to get ugly.

Scar Face approached Jade as his brother and the girls watched. He was loosening the belt on his trousers and telling Jade to start getting her clothes off.

Jade thought, as he did, that she would have to deal with him, but she didn't plan on the outcome he desired. She moved back half a step from facing the girls, swinging her right foot back a bit, squaring her feet, allowing Scar Face to think she was frightened.

CHAPTER FIFTY-EIGHT

Rick had arranged for himself, two of his men, and Matt to rendezvous with a small outboard boat with an electric motor at a point about a hundred meters up the coast from the target. Then they moved along the coast on the small boat to a landing at the back of the house where his men had tracked Jade's GPS signal. There were lights on within the house but it was dark in back, with no signs of activity, so they decided to come at the house from that direction. Matt could see the running lights of a large cabin cruiser bobbing in the water about a couple of hundred yards offshore. Rick had pointed it out. It was standing by waiting to be called in.

Rick turned to Matt. "I have four men in the front of the house. They will start shooting as soon as we reach the back door and I tell them go. Our guys in front will engage any shooters in the front of the house while we ensure no one is coming out the back. If no one comes out the back, we will go into the house and engage the Shui Fong guys from behind while their attention is focused on the problem in the front."

Matt just nodded. He was ready go. He had let Jade and the girls down. This was his chance to redeem himself. Hopefully they were not too late.

The door from the boat house leading up to the back of the house was open. Rick led the way moving up to the back door, Matt moved with him. He paused as they neared the house and listened carefully but heard no noise from within.

Rick positioned the other two men away from the door and towards two back windows. He spoke one word into the phone.

"Go."

Immediately, to the front of the house, Matt could hear the brrp, brrp, brrp of silenced automatic weapons breaking windows, shredding wood and bouncing bullets off stone walls. The initial burst of fire was followed by a moment or two of silence and then Matt heard yelling and answering automatic weapons fire from within the house. Rick and Matt each took a step back and to the side of the door. Anyone coming out would be coming soon.

The exchange of gunfire from the front continued and then Rick nodded to Matt, "Let's go."

Rick kicked in the door and went first covered by Matt. Matt joined him in a kitchen area. It was dark and empty. They both moved towards an entry way which led to a corridor leading to the front of the house. The gunfire rose in volume as they went further in.

They passed a stairway leading to the second floor and then came to the entry way leading to the front of the house. Rick glanced back to see that his men were with them. They were there, following closely, guns up, prepared to fire.

Rick and Matt took two more steps and had a clear view of the front interior room of the building. There were two triad men at each of the two windows, taking turns stepping up and shooting out. They had turned out the lights in the room but were visible from the lights outside. Rick held up four fingers to the men behind him so they would understand there were four enemy shooters ahead. He and Matt crawled forward, Rick pointing his gun to the left and Matt to the right side. Rick nodded, looking at Matt, and then opened fire on the two triad men on the left side and Matt did the same, firing toward the two triad men on the right side. One man on each side slumped down. With a panicky look, the second man on Matt's side whirled spraying fire back up the hallway to the kitchen. The shots went over the heads of Rick and Matt sprawled on the floor but Matt heard a grunt behind him. One of Rick's guys had been hit. Now Matt and Rick and the men behind them opened fire on the remaining two triad men. Both fell to the floor, laying still. The shooting from outside continued and then stopped as the men out front understood no one was shooting back.

Rick turned back to see how bad the man behind him had been hit. Matt yelled to him, "I'm going upstairs to see who's there." Rick, busy putting pressure on the wound of his man who had been shot, just nodded and then motioned to the other man to follow Matt up the stairs.

Matt moved up the stairs with his gun to the front, moving slowly just in case there was another shooter on the second floor.

CHAPTER FIFTY-NINE

As Scar Face moved towards her, Jade now stood her ground waiting. She had an advantage. He was not in a fighting mode, rather his mind was fixed on other matters. That was Jade's advantage. He started to reach out for her, his pants falling around his knees and Jade took her opportunity. She took a quick step forward with her left foot and hit him in the stomach with her right fist with all the force she could muster. He expelled air with a loud whoosh sound and doubled over. She grabbed the back of his head to hold it in place and kicked up as hard as she could with her right knee, breaking his nose and splattering blood over both of them. Jade held him up and looked over his shoulder at his brother who was looking on in disbelief.

Then the gunfire broke out in the front of the house. The younger brother paused, should he go to help his brother or see to the shooting? He looked towards the chair with the guns on it and Jade could see that she couldn't let him reach the guns. With both hands on his shoulder, holding him up, Jade propelled Scar Face back towards the chair, reaching it at the same time as the younger brother. They collided into each other, falling down over the chair, knocking the guns to the floor. Jade had let go of Scar Face who was now lying on the floor semiconscious. To her right she could see one of the handguns, she scrabbled for it, conscious that on the other side of the chair the younger brother was doing the same, grabbing for the second gun.

He grabbed the gun and stood up swinging to fire at Jade. She was still lying on the floor looking up at him but had a gun ready in her hand. They both fired but Jade fired first, two rounds hitting the younger brother center mass. He toppled over, falling across the upset chair.

Jade stayed down for a second trying to collect herself. There was a bang on the door and she heard someone yelling in English. She waited, on her back, head up, aiming towards the door, as a handgun was slowly poked into the room. Then a head appeared scanning the room. It was Matt, looking at the bodies and Jade with an incredulous look on his face.

Jade, with splotchs of Scar Face's blood on her shirt and face, smiled at Matt. She dropped her gun and leaning her head back to the floor. She was looking at the ceiling when she said to him, "Hey knuckledragger, what the hell took you so long?"

CHAPTER SIXTY

The dinner was Noi's idea. She and Matt had enjoyed a few days celebrating their reunion. Today was meant to be a family gathering with their new friend, Jade. It was not intended to mark the success of the mission but rather the ending of it. Matt had explained how the mission had expanded in progressive stages with each stage demanding more of Matt and Jade. The two had extended themselves, gained respect for each other and found a base of partnership they hadn't expected. Noi had no problem with that and thought it would be good to just eat good food, relax together and, in a manner, welcome Jade as someone in their private circle.

Jade understood Noi's intent and gave the get together a bit of an unexpected twist when she asked if she could bring along her friend. As Noi said yes she thought, well, this should be interesting.

Matt also found it interesting in the sense that it showed that Jade had accepted their recent partnership by being willing to open up some of her private life to them.

They had arranged the meeting at one of Matt and Noi's favorite meal spots. It was the You & Mee restaurant on the lower level of the Hyatt Erawan hotel, in the space between the hotel and the adjacent department store, which was also occupied by a wine bar and the Hyatt bakery. The special meal was one called Khao Soi Chiang Mai, noodles as they were prepared in the northern city. A meal they had shared and enjoyed often early in their relationship.

Matt and Noi were early and had a table when Jade appeared from the parking lot entrance at the back of the hotel. Holding hands with Jade was a Thai lady of medium height and slender build. She wore her long charcoal hair in the classic Thai style, combed straight back and falling almost to her waist. She was dressed in black form fitting slacks and a blue silk blouse with the top button open. She was strikingly beautiful with large almond eyes, high cheekbones, full reddened lips, and of coffee au lait skin color. She was definitely not one of the color obsessed 'Bangkok white girls' whose laser focus on achieving the whitest possible skin color Matt detested.

It was Noi, not Matt, who said, "Wow" as the couple walked through the doorway and headed towards their table.

Matt turned and looked and also wanted to say wow but the couple was too close now for Jade not to notice. He stayed silent and just nodded to Jade and her 'lady friend.'

"We're glad you could make it. Please have a seat."

Jade, who had a new hair look with a partial buzz cut on the side of her head which included a lightening flash design, paused, looked at her friend with a proprietary smile, and then said, "Matt and Noi, this is my friend, Lynn. I'm sorry we're a bit behind. Lynn took me over to visit the spirit tree, the shrine to the Goddess Tubtim on Soi Somkid, it's part of the Nai Lert park grounds. Have you been there?"

Matt nodded and turning to Noi explained, "The old spirit tree shrine was recently moved from behind the Swiss hotel due to the planned construction. You know it's a shrine for women wanting children, and lovers leaving love locks on the frame-work of the tree."

Noi raised her eyebrows at him, paused a second, and asked, "Why haven't you taken me to see it?"

Jade laughed and looked at her lady friend. Matt had walked right into it. It was going to be fun down the road, watching him dance around questions like this.

ACKNOWLEDGMENTS

I must acknowledge the patience and brilliant help of the world's best editor, Elaine Ash; the thorough readings and comments of Chris Maxwell; and the chopper pilot/military woman warrior input from Pearl Phaovisaid.

Tom Crowley's origins are in the Midwest American town of Milwaukee, although virtually his entire adult life has been spent living in Asia in positions with the military, diplomatic corps and business until the Asian financial crash of 1997. Living in Thailand at that time he decided to explore a different path in life and volunteered at the Mercy Centre in Bangkok, an NGO working to shelter and educate street children. Tom has continued with the foundation to this time.

His writing reflects his varied experiences living and working in Asia. He divides his time between homes in Kensington, Maryland and Bangkok. His recreation is competing in pool tournaments and league play. His two adult children and wife reside in the U.S.

BOOKS

On the following pages are a few
more great titles from the
Down & Out Books publishing family.

For a complete list of books and to
sign up for our newsletter,
go to DownAndOutBooks.com.

Third Degree
Ross Klavan, Tim O'Mara and Charles Salzberg

Down & Out Books
October 2020
978-1-64396-162-0

Cut Loose All Those Who Drag You Down by Ross Klavan. A crooked reporter who fronts for the mob is in deep trouble and it's clear somebody is going to pay with his life.

Beaned by Tim O'Mara. Aggie discovers a sinister plot to exploit what some consider a precious commodity: the trafficking of under-aged children for the purposes of sex.

The Fifth Column by Charles Salzberg. A young reporter uncovers that the recently disbanded German-American Bund might still be active and is planning a number of dangerous actions on American soil.

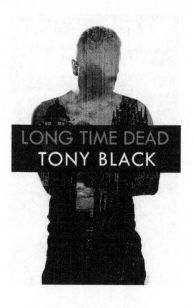

Long Time Dead
A Gus Dury Novel
Tony Black

Down & Out Books
November 2020
978-1-64396-118-7

Gus Dury is back on the drink.

While in hospital after a hit-and-run accident, his best friend, Hod, asks him to investigate the ritual, on-campus hanging of an Edinburgh University student. Few of the students are prepared to talk about it—until another one of their group turns up dead by the same method.

But Gus now moves into very dangerous waters as he begins to discover what and who is really behind it all—and he becomes the next target for the executioner.

All Due Respect 2020
Chris Rhatigan & David Nemeth, editors

All Due Respect, an imprint of
Down & Out Books
November 2020
978-1-64396-165-1

Twelve short stories from the top writers in crime fiction today.

Featuring the work of Stephen D. Rogers, Tom Leins, Michael Pool, Andrew Davie, Sharon Diane King, Preston Lang, Jay Butkowski, Steven Berry, Craig Francis Coates, Bobby Mathews, Michael Penncavage, and BV Lawson.

Deemer's Inlet
Stephen Burdick

Shotgun Honey, an imprint of
Down & Out Books
August 2020
978-1-64396-104-0

Far from the tourist meccas of Ft. Lauderdale and Miami Beach, a chief of police position in the quiet, picturesque town of Deemer's Inlet on the Gulf coast of Florida seemed ideal for Eldon Quick—until the first murder.

The crime and a subsequent killing force Quick to call upon his years of experience as a former homicide detective in Miami. Soon after, two more people are murdered and Quick believes a serial killer is on the loose. As Quick works to uncover the identity and motive of the killer, he must contend with an understaffed police force, small town politics, and curious residents.